Breaking Negative Thinking Patterns Step by Step

Breaking Negative Thinking Patterns Step by Step

A Systematic Plan to Change Unwanted Feelings, Thoughts and Behaviour

Hannie van Genderen

Originally published by uitgeverij Nieuwezijds, Amsterdam under the title *Doorbreek je patronen in vijf stappen.*

Illustrations: © Inge Voets

Published by John Wiley & Sons, Inc., Hoboken, New Jersey.

For general information on our other products and services or for technical support, please contact our Customer Care Department within the United States at (800) 762-2974, outside the United States at (317) 572-3993 or fax (317) 572-4002.

Wiley also publishes its books in a variety of electronic formats. Some content that appears in print may not be available in electronic formats. For more information about Wiley products, visit our web site at www.wiley.com.

Library of Congress Cataloging-in-Publication Data applied for:
ISBN: 9781394360352

Cover Design: Wiley
Cover Images: © Nguyen Kim Phuong/Shutterstock, © Kuznetsov Alexey/Shutterstock, © AlexandraRooss/stock.adobe.com

Set in 11/14pts Minion by Straive, Pondicherry, India

Printed and bound by CPI Group (UK) Ltd, Croydon, CR0 4YY

C9781394360352_040626

Contents

List of exercises

Preface

The book *Breaking Negative Thinking Patterns*, which I cowrote with my colleagues Gitta Jacob and Laura Seebauer, has been an extraordinary success: in 10 years, the Dutch-language edition has sold over 200,000 copies. The book has been translated into 10 languages. Since its publication, there have been a number of developments that led to the writing of this new book.

Over the years, I often received questions from clients who are in schema therapy and from people who have used it as a self-help book. Some wondered whether there might be more ways to change modes, break patterns. Others told me they had different modes and pitfalls (schemas) than were described in *Breaking Negative Thinking Patterns*. People also wondered how pitfalls could lead to modes and details about the process of changing modes from start to finish. What should you do first and what can only happen later in the process?

Treatment methodologies were improved and refined in clinical practice and in light of scientific research at various sites in the Netherlands. It also became increasingly clear that treatment consisted of various phases. In this book, I divide this into five phases or five steps to break your negative patterns. The role of the person helping you (a therapist or a close friend) changes with you at each stage.

An international working group led by Prof. Arnoud Arntz and Prof. Marleen Rijkeboer (Arntz et al., 2021) has considered these kinds of questions and came up with some interesting new insights into the relationship between basic needs, pitfalls (schemas) and modes (patterns). Their research led to the discovery of a number of new pitfalls and modes, each of which has been incorporated into this new book. The term 'coping style' (survival strategy) was also defined differently. Originally, the terms fight, flight and freeze (as a reaction to an external threat) were used to define Overcompensation, Avoidance and Surrender. But according to this working group, it is not about an external threat, but about the internal reaction to the activation of a pitfall. Because of this, the term 'coping style' is now preferred to 'survival strategy' and 'coping mode' to 'survival mode'. You can still deal with your pitfall in three different ways, but the content and one of the names of the concepts has changed: Inversion is acting as if the opposite of your pitfall is true, Avoidance is acting as if the pitfall is not there and Surrender is acting as if your pitfall is true. We explain how this affects the formation of modes in detail.

In *Breaking Negative Thinking Patterns*, you learn which modes you can develop and recognise in yourself and others. We discuss many examples of people with unhelpful modes, whereby you discover how they work. It does describe some exercises to change your modes, but it does not systematically explain how that process works or in what steps. This new book does just that, based on a five-step plan to change your modes. Further, the latest insights in the relationship between basic needs, pitfalls, coping styles and modes are clearly explained.

To write this new book, I drew a lot of inspiration first and foremost from the work of Arnoud Arntz and Marleen Rijkeboer. Not only have they done a lot of research on schema therapy, but we have also enjoyed teaching in this field together. The intensive collaboration in knowledge sharing with my colleagues Remco van der Wijngaart and Hélène Bögels was also very valuable to me. They read the first versions of this book and provided meaningful comments for which I owe them my thanks. I thank my colleague Truus Kersten for her contribution to launching the book. I would also like to thank my partner Jos Halfens and brother-in-law Igor van de Wal who read along as interested laymen, and Dianne Nijhoff who encouraged me to embark on this project and stick with it. Last but not least, I am indebted to NC, a former client, who provided meaningful feedback on the book from her own experience.

Hannie van Genderen
September 2023

1

Introduction

Getting angry at yourself when something fails. Panicking when your partner goes on a business trip for a few days. Being completely beside yourself when a friend cancels an appointment. These reactions are too intense and if you exhibit them relatively often, this forms a pattern called a mode.

Modes are aspects of our personality that formed due to (difficult) circumstances in our youth. These can be healthy patterns of feelings, thoughts and behaviour (helpful modes) or unhealthy patterns (unhelpful modes). In this book, you will discover how to recognise unhelpful modes and change them into helpful modes – either by yourself or with the guidance of a therapist.

The five steps

This book offers a systematic five-step plan for changing modes. We follow three people (Sarah, Martin and Nora) who each go through the five steps in their own way and succeed in breaking their modes.

This book contains the latest insights (Arntz et al., 2021) into the relationship between basic needs, pitfalls (schemas) and modes (patterns), as well as some newly discovered pitfalls and modes. I also discuss the effectiveness of different treatment options and explain what you, as a client, can expect from your therapist, what obstacles could arise during therapy and how to maintain the results of change in the future. Through the stories of three people, you can follow how they complete these steps and how they succeed in breaking their patterns.

After a general chapter on modes and pitfalls, the step-by-step programme begins, and you learn to figure out for yourself which modes you are struggling with, where they come from and how to handle them when you are confronted with them. This process of change takes time and energy, so take your time. Do the steps in the order they are presented, and only move on to the next when you feel you have sufficiently mastered a step.

Step 1:   *Discovering your own modes (Chapter 3)*
The first step is to identify your own modes. By describing them, you understand them better, you can reflect on them, and you are less likely to be swept away by them. You will gain a sharper insight into how your problems originated and how they affect many situations in your life now.

Step 2:   *Recognising modes in everyday situations (Chapter 4)*
The second step teaches you to recognise that you are reacting from one of your modes in everyday situations where you feel annoyed. In this step, you also start to understand the experiences in your childhood to which these modes are related, and what basic needs were insufficiently met, or even went unmet, at that time.

Step 3:   *Starting to change modes (Chapter 5)*
In the third step, you will use concrete exercises to break your modes. The exercises seem simple, but you will find that modes are remarkably persistent. Because of this, you need to repeat the exercises multiple times to see results. You can certainly use some help with this from others.

Step 4:   *Changing your modes independently (Chapter 6)*
The fourth step teaches you how to change your modes independently and translate them into different behaviour. Your unhelpful modes get weaker and weaker and you develop more and more helpful modes.

Step 5:   *Continuing to change modes in the future (Chapter 7)*
The fifth step is about how you can maintain the changes you have achieved into the future. Your helpful modes are now at the forefront. When you face difficulties in your life, old modes may re-emerge. The important thing is that you recognise this early and draw on what you learnt in the previous steps and respond from your helpful modes.

In the book, we follow Sarah, Martin and Nora as they go through all the steps of the process. Sarah gets to work independently because she does not have a personality disorder, but she does have persistent patterns that she wants to change. Martin and Nora are supported by a schema therapist because they do have a personality disorder. These three fictional people are compiled from the stories of the countless clients I have seen over the past 40 years, and they cannot be traced back to specific individuals. The problems these three struggle with are common, but most of the tips are perfectly applicable, even if your problems are a little bit different.

Each of these chapters includes a description of your goals in this phase and exercises with examples from the lives of Sarah, Martin and Nora. There are also tips on how you can overcome difficult moments in this process of change.

The final chapter, which summarises all the information and insights, is followed by appendices with worksheets that you can also download from https://www.wiley.com/go/breakingnegative patterns/1e.

Introducing: Sarah, Martin and Nora

Sarah

Sarah is 36 and has a brother who is three years younger. She is married, has two children (aged four and six) and works as an economics teacher at a college. She also lectures on her subject and collaborates in projects within the college aimed at developing new teaching modules and academic research. In her spare time, she volunteers at a couple of associations. She is active in the neighbourhood committee, serves on the board of the rowing club and, as a parent, often helps out with extra activities at her children's school. Her husband also works very hard. He sometimes complains that they don't spend enough time together but seems resigned to that. All their energy goes to work and the children.

Upbringing

Sarah's father is a physics teacher, her mother a nurse. She says her relationship with her parents is reasonably good, but she does not see them very often. She has a good relationship with her younger brother. He has more problems with work and relationships than she does, and Sarah doesn't quite understand why things in his life go wrong so often.

Sarah's parents also always worked very hard. They put a heavy emphasis on performance and success. 'Deeds not words' was the motto. They had firm views on how you should live your life and ingrained in their children that you should always fulfil your duties before you can have fun. In practice, then, there wasn't much room for fun. Emotions didn't get much attention either. Sarah was on her own when she was struggling. As a result, she started sharing less and less with her parents. That is one of the reasons why she has only superficial contact with them now.

Her younger brother was slightly less able to keep up at school than Sarah and got a lot of criticism for that. There was also a period when he was bullied at school, and he didn't get good help with that from the teachers or his parents. They felt he needed to stick up for himself more. This resulted in him not completing his further education. Overall, he is a typical case of a jack of all trades, master of none. This means he has developed different modes than Sarah with the same kind of upbringing.

Symptoms and problems

Sarah constantly feels like she is pushing herself to the limit and often suffers from impostor syndrome. She is worried that she could burn out. Despite this fear, she continues to pursue all her activities. She still wants to keep doing everything as well as possible, otherwise she'll feel like a failure. When something doesn't go quite right, she is critical of herself. Otherwise, she doesn't talk about her problems much and thinks she shouldn't complain.

She does have a few friends, but she doesn't spend much time with them. It's as if she doesn't need love and friendship. When she is stressed, she seeks distraction by watching series or surfing the internet. Somehow she realises that her husband is right when he says she works too hard, but she doesn't know how to do otherwise. She frequently feels lonely. Sometimes she gets angry with herself or others when she feels she's letting them put too much pressure on her. However, most of the time she does her best to do everything very well.

Sarah decides she still wants to change something about her patterns and wants to start doing this on her own using the steps described in this book.

Martin

Fifty-four-year-old Martin works as an administrative assistant in a notary's office. After completing senior general secondary education, he didn't know what he wanted to do. His mother arranged for him to work in a notary's office. He was married to a rather dominant woman who determined almost everything for him. They have an 18-year-old son. Ten years ago, he divorced his wife when it emerged that she was secretly in another relationship. In the divorce, she got the house and almost all its contents because Martin felt his son should be able to continue living in the parental home. Since the divorce, he has been sharing a flat with an old friend. He sees this friend as his anchor. He likes his work but sometimes has problems with his colleagues and supervisor because they always have him do extra work and he doesn't dare to say no. Everyone seems to assume that Martin is always there for everyone. When he isn't, some react negatively to it. Fearing rejection, he does not express his dissatisfaction and adapts to others.

Martin has many physical complaints, such as stomach-aches and headaches, and is often tired, but medical examination cannot explain his symptoms. His housemate does support him and arranges a lot for him when it's all too much for him. When his roommate has to go away for a few days for work, Martin feels alone and kills time with gaming and sleeping. He has rather few friends.

Upbringing

Martin is the youngest of three children. His parents were over-protective in his childhood and saw danger everywhere. His father worked in a garage but went on disability quite young due to mental and physical problems. He was very dominant and wanted everything to be perfect and to go his way. He was not very emotionally involved with the children. Still, he was very helpful. Martin was not encouraged to do anything himself, and what he did do on his own initiative was frowned upon. His mother was sweet and caring but also insecure. Mostly, she accommodated what his father wanted. She worried a lot about Martin's sister, who was often ill and needed a lot of care. Martin's older brother used to have many conflicts with his father because he did dare to speak his mind and did what he wanted.

Martin's father died a few years ago. The loss of his father was very difficult for Martin. His mother is not coping well with the loss of her husband and has depressive symptoms. She often leans on Martin. Martin's brother is a successful and hardworking businessman. He is married and has two children. Martin doesn't see him very often, and he has the impression that his brother just thinks he's annoying. His sister always remained living with her parents. She is an anchor for their mother and often for Martin as well. He has a good connection with her. Some of Martin's sister's modes are similar to his, but his brother developed different modes because he was more inclined to take on the conflict with their father.

Symptoms and problems

Martin was referred to a psychologist by his doctor because extensive medical examination did not reveal a cause for his physical problems. Martin went to him almost every week and kept asking for a solution to his issues. The doctor always managed to reassure him but only temporarily.

Martin faithfully attends appointments with his psychologist but is not very clear on what he wants help with. He wants to be rid of his symptoms and asks the counsellor for advice. He has little confidence in his own abilities and feels guilty about leaning on his roommate and sister so much. At the same time, he thinks others can do everything better than him, so he keeps asking them for advice. At work, he shuns contact with colleagues. He often fears doing something wrong.

The psychologist has told him that he has dependent and avoidant personality disorder and suggests focusing treatment on that.

Nora

Nora is a 25-year-old woman and currently holds irregular jobs as a cleaner or shop assistant. She has been living with her boyfriend Frank for three years. He doesn't have a permanent job either. The two often argue, with both shouting and saying hurtful things to each other. Nora has many acquaintances but only one significant friend.

Nora is often anxious and depressed. She drinks too much and smokes cannabis regularly. Nora has very low self-esteem and doubts about her abilities. She has not completed further education, although she is quite intelligent. Because of her insecurity, she avoids social activities, making her feel lonely. When she cannot avoid social contact, she acts tougher than she is. As a result, she sometimes comes across as arrogant and this kind of contact exhausts her.

Upbringing

Nora grew up in a family with two brothers and a sister. Her father was a domineering, aggressive man who drank too much. Without alcohol, he was only verbally aggressive, but when he was drunk, blows were frequent. Nora occasionally answered back to him, but that only led to even more trouble. He thought she was a difficult child.

Her mother was a gentle and kind, but also anxious and submissive, housewife. Fearing her husband, she kept quiet and did not protect the children from him. After father's outbursts, she always tried to calm the situation. She typically used statements like: 'Ah, you know him' and 'Just keep quiet, because if you go against it you'll only make it worse'. When it all got too much for her, she would sometimes go to her family for a few days. This was very frightening for Nora because she never knew if and when her mother would return. Her mother couldn't handle it all very well and often called on Nora to help her, both in the household and with the problems with her father.

Nora has always felt lonely and different from others. People around them regarded their family as strange and many people were afraid of her father. At school, she was an outsider. She did not dare to invite other children to her home because she was ashamed of her father. She was actually a capable learner but did have concentration problems. This, combined with the problems at home, ultimately prevented her from obtaining a high school diploma.

Symptoms and problems

Nora is seeking help now that she's been fired for the umpteenth time and the arguments with Frank are increasingly getting out of hand. However, she does not dare to break up with him because she cannot bear to be alone. Nora has major problems with mood swings, harms herself and has already attempted suicide once, at a time when she was really at her wit's end.

A psychologist has treated her anxiety symptoms before, but that didn't help much. She doubts that she will benefit from the help now because she actually thinks she is a hopeless case. The psychologist who treated her anxiety symptoms tells her she has borderline personality disorder and refers her to a schema therapist.

2

What are modes and pitfalls?

In our youth, we develop under vastly different circumstances. Aside from our unique hereditary predisposition, our upbringing plays an important role. But influences from outside the family, such as our experiences at school, sports teams or other clubs, are also important. There are four key concepts in our development into adults: *basic needs*, *pitfalls* (schemas), *coping styles* and *modes* (patterns). We discuss these four concepts and their interrelationships in more detail in this chapter.

How do modes arise?

People who are stuck in certain areas of their lives have unhelpful modes at the forefront. These are negative states of mind or stubborn character traits that crop up every time you experience difficulty. Unhelpful modes may arise because the *basic needs* of a child are not, or not sufficiently, met. The result is that, as a child, you develop certain negative thoughts and feelings about yourself and others. For example, if you are always criticised, you start thinking you're stupid and bad and feel worthless and dejected. This is how you develop *pitfalls* (schemas), which you carry with you your whole life. Combined with the strategies you learnt as a child to avoid feeling the pain of that lack too strongly (coping styles), unhealthy modes form.

To give you an insight into the emergence of modes, I start by describing the basic needs everyone has, and then what pitfalls you can develop, what possible *coping styles* there are, and finally how they lead to *modes*.

Basic needs and pitfalls

Children have various *basic needs*. First of all, they need a secure, loving and predictable bond with others (*acceptance, connection, safety* and *predictability*) and the feeling that they have some capability (*competence*). They also have the need to become independent from their parents (*autonomy* and *identity*) and need the freedom to express feelings and opinions (*self-expression*) and to play and have fun (*spontaneity, play* and *relaxation*). Finally, they also need boundaries and adequate self-control (*realistic limits* and *self-control*), as well as fair treatment (*fairness*). Taken together, this should lead to what is known in the field as 'self-coherence': a coherent picture of who they are and how the world works (*coherent image of yourself and of the world*). The basic needs are described in Table 2.1.

If these needs were insufficiently met, for example because parents or other caregivers were unable to meet them, children are unfulfilled and develop negative feelings and thoughts, which can still trouble them in later life. These kinds of deficits can also arise because children experience serious issues, for example losing loved ones or being bullied or abused. You could think of it as emotional bruising that hurts again when touched again later in life: they are negative feelings and thoughts about yourself, others and the world, or *pitfalls*.

The unfulfilled basic needs (deficits) are linked to 21 pitfalls, which in turn translate into 21 negative mindsets (see Table 2.1).

When you repeatedly get negative messages, feel threatened, abused or experience other unpleasant things, you develop persistent (negative) views about yourself, others and the world. You start believing in them more and more. That also leads to negative emotions and unpleasant physical sensations such as abdominal pain or tightness in the chest. A pitfall is therefore a kind of lens through which you look at reality. As we have mentioned, you can also look at pitfalls as emotional bruises. When you bump against them, you are flooded with negative emotions. When all these basic needs do get fulfilled to a sufficient degree, of course you don't develop pitfalls, but healthy, helpful modes.

Table 2.1 How do unfulfilled basic needs (deficits) lead to pitfalls?

Deficits	Leads to pitfall	Mindset
Lack of acceptance, connection, security and predictability	Mistrust/abuse	No one can be trusted. Others will take advantage of me, cheat, manipulate or humiliate me.
	Abandonment/ instability	Everyone lets me down sooner or later. I can't assume that others will really support me or be there for me when I need them.
	Social isolation/ alienation	I don't belong. I am very different from other people. In groups, I'm always an outsider.
	Emotional deprivation	No one loves me or understands me. I will not get attention, warmth, good advice or care from others. They don't listen to me and I can't share my feelings with them. I am on my own.
	Defectiveness/shame	I am inwardly bad and worthless. I am unattractive. If others really get to know me, they will also find out and reject me. I am ashamed of myself.
Lack of autonomy, competence and identity	Dependence/ incompetence	I am helpless and dependent on others. I can't handle daily things. I need help from others in making decisions or when I have to do something new.
	Failure	I can't do anything. I am stupid and have no talent for anything. I am unable to perform as well as my peers in education, work or sports.
	Vulnerability to harm or illness	There is danger everywhere. Something terrible could happen to me or the people I care about at any moment. I'm afraid that I'll get ill or that a disaster will happen. When things go wrong, I don't know how to help myself or others.

	Enmeshment/ entanglement	I am overly involved with my parents and family. I do everything the same as them and don't know who I am or what I want. When no one is around, I feel alone and aimless.
Lack of self-expression (expressing your opinions and feelings)	Subjugation	I always have to obey or I will be punished. I have to suppress my needs and feelings to avoid conflicts and negative reactions.
	Self-sacrifice	I always have to take care of others and put my own needs second. If I don't, I feel guilty. I gain self-esteem by helping others.
	Approval and recognition seeking	I can't manage without attention, approval and recognition. I value status and good looks to gain social regard. This is often at the expense of my own needs or development.
Lack of realistic limits and self-control	Entitlement (grandiosity)	I am superior to most people. I don't have to follow the rules that apply to the rest. I can do whatever I want without considering the effect on others. I like to have power and control over others.
	Lack of self-discipline and self-control	I cannot contain my feelings and impulses, so I do everything impulsively. I cannot handle frustrations. I don't like obligations. I can't stand discomforts such as pain or arguments. If I have to make an effort or do a boring task, I give up. I cannot wait for a long-term reward.
Lack of spontaneity, play and relaxation (excessive control)	Negativity/pessimism	Everything always goes wrong anyway. I always have bad luck. I only see the negative side of things and dismiss the positive side. I am often worried and on guard. I complain to others a lot.
	Emotional inhibition	I always hold back all my emotions and impulses because they could harm others and/or that they will leave me. If I don't restrain my emotions, I could lose self-esteem and I would feel ashamed of myself. I prefer to approach everything rationally.

(Continued)

Table 2.1 (Continued)

Deficits	Leads to pitfall	Mindset
	High demands (unrelenting standards/overly critical)	I have to do everything perfectly and can't make any mistakes. I can never do well enough, because there is always room for improvement. So I have to try harder. I'm critical of myself, but also of others. I want everything to be well organised and done efficiently and on time. This often comes at the expense of fun, relaxation and my health. Contact with family or friends always comes second.
	Punitiveness	People should be punished harshly for their mistakes. I am impatient, intolerant and rarely forgive mistakes, regarding both myself and others.
Lack of fairness	Unfairness/dishonesty	I can't stand dishonesty or unfairness. Actions by those who behave dishonestly are not addressed. I'm always taken advantage of and can't do anything about it.
Lack of a coherent picture of yourself and of the world	Confusion about who you are (incoherent identity)	I am confused. I do not experience myself as a whole. I have lost my grip on myself and am made up of unconnected parts. I don't know who I am and I feel lost.
	Confusion about how the world works (lack of a meaningful world)	Not only have I lost a grip on myself, I also have no grip on the world. I don't understand how the world works. Everything seems to keep changing, and I feel alienated from the things happening around me. I am afraid of existence because I don't understand what is happening and what it means.

These persistent negative ideas about yourself, others and the world play a continuous background role in your life. Sometimes it is not very noticeable, but as soon as something unpleasant occurs in your life related to those horrible experiences, your pitfall is activated. In other words, you automatically fall into your pitfall because that's what you've learnt.

For example, if you have the pitfall of Failure, it is not as active when things are going well. But then when something goes wrong, you suddenly feel like a failure. You think: everything always goes wrong for me, and you feel dejected. You're unable to put things into perspective and to realise that everyone makes mistakes from time to time – let alone feel the emotional space to realise that you can learn from them. Let's take a look at how deficits in their upbringing affect Sarah, Martin and Nora.

Deficits in upbringing: unmet basic needs

Sarah's parents put too much emphasis on performance and rules. There wasn't much room for fun. Because of this, Sarah had a deficit in spontaneity, play and relaxation. For her, this led to the pitfalls of Negativity/ Pessimism, Emotional Inhibition, High Demands and Punitiveness. Because her parents only paid attention to performance, there was little regard for her emotions. As a result, she also has the pitfall of Emotional Deprivation.

Martin's parents didn't give him much room to explore his own potential or develop his own preferences and opinions. His father's will was law, and his mother was very insecure and anxious. As a result, he experienced a deficit in self-expression, which led to the pitfalls of Subjugation, Self-sacrifice and Approval/Recognition Seeking. On top of that, Martin also had a deficit in autonomy, competence and a sense of identity, which led to the pitfalls of Dependence/Incompetence, Failure, Vulnerability to Harm and Illness and Enmeshment/Entanglement.

Nora's parents were unpredictable. There was a constant danger that her father would flare up in anger or that her mother would disappear. Nora had difficulty concentrating and was treated as a difficult child. At school, she was an outsider. She was often lonely.

As a result, Nora experienced a lack of acceptance, connection, safety and predictability, which led to the pitfalls of Mistrust/Abuse, Abandonment/Instability, Social Isolation/ Alienation, Emotional Deprivation and Inferiority/Shame. She also lacked boundaries and self-control, which in her case resulted in the pitfall of Lack of Self-Discipline/Self-Control.

She was also somewhat lacking in a few other areas, which is why she also suffers from the pitfalls of Failure and Dependence/Incompetence.

It might seem, with 21, that there are quite a lot of pitfalls, but fortunately most people did not grow up in such difficult circumstances that they had deficits in all areas. Or perhaps they did lack something, but not to such an extent that it left them with serious psychological problems. Furthermore, an upbringing with deficits is more harmful to some children than others. The effects depend on things like predisposition, temperament, sensitivity and intelligence. Support figures outside the family or positive experiences can also protect a child from negative long-term consequences.

However, if you experienced severe deficits in having your basic needs met, you could develop a personality disorder. The word 'disorder' means that those pitfalls and modes affect you so much that they seriously disrupt your daily life. Not only do you then struggle with intense thoughts and feelings, but you also exhibit behaviour that is awkward or even harmful to yourself and sometimes to others. However, that does not mean you can't do anything about it. This book is therefore written for people with milder problems (using Sarah as an example), as well as for people who had major deficits and need professional help to deal with their modes (using Martin and Nora as examples). For both groups, I describe what you can do to change it, with or without a therapist. See the text box about schema therapy on page 22.

Coping styles

To avoid suffering too much from childhood deficits and the resulting pitfalls, you develop forms of behaviour early in life to deal with that lack, and with the unpleasant thoughts and feelings triggered by the pitfall. We then call these *coping styles*. When coping styles become ingrained, they combine with pitfalls to form modes: persistent patterns of feelings, thoughts and behaviour, or aspects of our personality, that become active in difficult circumstances to save you from the dire situation (see Figure 2.1). Coping styles were created at difficult times in your childhood as a stopgap measure to survive (they are also referred to as 'survival strategies'). Unfortunately, the coping styles that were once so

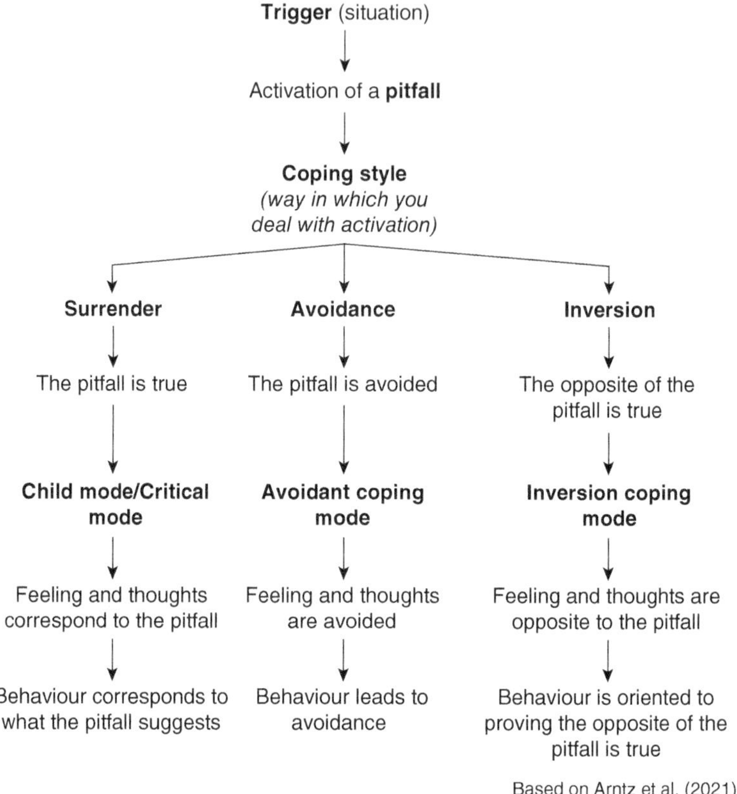

Figure 2.1   The origins of unhelpful modes

useful often actually become obstacles later in life. There are three coping styles:

- *Resignation.* You take the (negative) feelings and thoughts about yourself to be completely true. You could also call it surrender. This means, for example, that you feel you really are bad, awkward, failed or dependent.
- *Avoidance.* You act as if those feelings and thoughts are not there by shutting them off or by seeking distraction, for example by working hard, denying your feelings or abusing numbing substances. You might make sure you don't stand out or avoid stressful situations.
- *Inversion.* The third possibility is that you deal with your thoughts and feelings by doing the exact opposite of what

they tell you or prescribe. This could be by acting exaggeratedly popular, funny, independent or tough, while you actually feel lonely, boring, dependent or vulnerable.

You can also alternate between these coping styles. For example, if you are invited to visit friends and you feel inferior, you completely surrender to that feeling by saying that what you think and do isn't important, and constantly saying sorry (resignation). You can also decide not to go, take liquid courage or shut off your feelings altogether (avoidance). The third alternative is to do the opposite of what your sense of defectiveness dictates, and instead pretend to be much better than you are, for example by bragging about your achievements and constantly seeking affirmation from others for this (inversion).

Modes

When you try to handle unpleasant thoughts and feelings through resignation, avoidance or inversion, different modes form: aspects of our personality.

In other words, a pitfall combined with one of the coping styles leads to a mode. For instance, resignation is a coping style that can lead to child modes or critical modes. And the coping styles of avoidance and inversion can lead to avoidant coping modes and inversion coping modes, respectively. When such a mode is activated, specific feelings, thoughts and behaviours coincide. And at another time, for example when another pitfall is involved, other feelings, thoughts and behaviours may be triggered, and you also enter a different mode. People around you therefore see one particular side of you in such a situation, and you don't usually realise that you then behave in a typical way.

When you map out for yourself what modes you have and where those aspects of your personality come from, you'll gain a better understanding of why you sometimes react unexpectedly awkwardly or come across as annoying. Or you'll see better why others don't always understand your behaviour, which often only makes it worse.

There are five types of modes that can play a role in your life: child modes, critical modes, coping modes, the healthy adult mode and the happy child mode. Child modes, critical modes and coping modes can cause problems and are therefore called *unhelpful* or *dysfunctional modes*. The healthy adult mode and the happy child mode are *helpful modes* and actually contribute to healthy development. Like everyone else, the three people we follow in this book have multiple modes (more about that in Chapter 3), but for now we will give an example of an unhelpful mode for each person here.

Unhelpful modes

Sarah's critical mode

Sarah is dissatisfied with her performance, even though people around her think it is good enough.

- *Feeling.* She is dissatisfied and stressed.
- *Thought.* I'm not doing it right.
- *Behaviour.* She will try even harder.

Martin's avoidant coping mode

Martin calls in sick after being given a new task that seems difficult to him.

- *Feeling.* He is fearful.
- *Thought.* I can't do that.
- *Behaviour.* He calls in sick so he does not have to do this task.

Nora's child mode

Nora is upset because her best friend Elly has called to reschedule an appointment.

- *Feeling.* She is sad and scared.
- *Thought.* Elly doesn't like me anymore.
- *Behaviour.* She reacts upset on the phone and starts crying.

Everyone has modes, but it makes a big difference whether you have strong unhelpful modes and weak helpful modes or the other way around. The more your life is dominated by a harsh critical voice in the back of your mind and violent emotional reactions from the child modes, the more strong, rigid and unhelpful coping modes you develop. You then get stuck in one or more areas of your life and have great difficulty in breaking these patterns. In that case, it is recommended to seek help from a schema therapist. You can find them at www.schematherapysociety.com. If you suffer from your modes to a lesser extent but would still like to change something, you can also do this on your own, or with the support of a close friend. Try to find someone who is willing to help you but who doesn't become too much of a 'social worker' for you. It should be someone with whom you also talk about and do other things.

What is schema therapy?

Schema therapy aims to change modes caused by pitfalls (maladaptive schemas) and coping styles. This is done by changing your feelings, thoughts and behaviour. The therapy not only focuses on problems in your current life, but also focuses on what you have experienced in the past. Schema therapy assumes that modes begin to develop early in your life. If you had many unpleasant or even traumatic experiences in your childhood, your therapist will help you process those experiences and give them a different meaning.

For example, if you were mistreated, abused or bullied, you may have come to believe that it is down to you and that you are a bad person. Your therapist will help you discover that you did nothing wrong but were treated wrong and will support you and teach you how to handle difficult situations differently.

Schema therapy uses various exercises to achieve this change:

- *Gaining new experiences.* The aim of experiential exercises is to help you feel better. For example, this is done by going back to the past in your imagination and experiencing what it's like to have someone support you in a difficult situation and what it's like to stand up to or even chase away people who treat you badly. You can also gain new experiences by talking about your problems with your therapist or with good friends and seeing that they understand and support you.
- *Changing thoughts.* To change your negative thoughts about yourself and others, learn to examine your thoughts by coming up with arguments for and against these ideas. Many (negative) thoughts were instilled in you in the past by caregivers or peers. Together with your therapist, you give a counterweight to these messages.

> • *Changing behaviour.* Once you feel different and think more positively about yourself, you will also start trying to change your behaviour. By practising how to communicate differently with people, you can develop better relationships and your needs for care, attention and recognition in your current life are better met.
>
> For practical information, see www.schematherapysociety.com

I will now start by explaining the five different unhelpful and helpful modes. In Chapter 2, I describe how you can map them out for yourself.

Unhelpful modes

If you had unpleasant experiences in childhood and/or if any basic needs were not met, you develop unhelpful modes that in your current life get you out of the frying pan into the fire. These modes cause you to react to others with either excessive emotion or excessive detachment, which increases the likelihood that people will not understand you, or reject you. Unfortunately, this amplifies those modes, making you feel worse and worse. The unhelpful modes can be classified as child modes, critical modes and coping modes.

Child modes

Everyone feels scared, angry, sad or defiant from time to time, but it is usually appropriate to the situation you're in and does not last long. If someone scolds you or lies to you, it is only natural to feel angry or sad because of that. But even then, you could try to respond maturely and not yell at or even hit that person. Sometimes you also do things on a whim or want to get your way, but you don't do that so much that it harms yourself or others.

However, if you become so overwhelmed by feelings such as hurt, sadness, anger, frustration or resentment that you seem to lose control of yourself, then you are in a child mode. And that is especially the case if the event really isn't all that serious, but you get upset or furious anyway. Your coping style is then complete surrender to your pitfalls, to the feeling you get when one or more of your basic needs are fundamentally violated. You believe that pitfall to be completely true.

For example, if your girlfriend unexpectedly cancels a date and this shakes you up completely, or you get so angry that you never want to see her again, you are reacting like a small child. This has then touched feelings that you experienced as a child and you're experiencing the pain of the past again. You immediately think: 'You see! Everyone does let me down!' This then points to the Abandonment/Instability pitfall (see Table 2.1). Or you think: 'You see, she doesn't like me anymore!' This could then be related to the Defectiveness/Shame pitfall.

A child mode is also referred to in practice as 'little [your own name]', 'little me' or 'the vulnerable child'.

Vulnerable child modes

When you zoom in on unmet basic needs, you can distinguish different child modes. Depending on the main things a person was deprived of in his or her childhood, the vulnerable child may have different child modes. The first column of Table 2.2 lists the six modes of the vulnerable child. The middle column describes the main deficits associated with this. The right-hand column gives the resulting pitfalls you might have for each type of vulnerable child mode. This doesn't mean that if you are in the abandoned, abused, disregarded, child mode, for example you have all five pitfalls associated with that deficit – but you may have more than one. For example, in this mode, one person might primarily feel distrustful, abused (Mistrust/Abuse) and abandoned (Abandonment/Instability), while another may feel that he is nothing (Defectiveness/

Table 2.2 Vulnerable child modes

Mode	Deficits	Potential pitfalls
Abandoned, abused, disregarded child	Lack of acceptance, connection, security and predictability	• Mistrust/abuse • Abandonment/ instability • Social isolation/ alienation • Emotional deprivation • Defectiveness/shame
Dependent, failing child	Lack of autonomy, competence and identity	Dependence/ incompetence • Failure • Vulnerability to harm and illness • Enmeshment/ entanglement
Subordinate child	Lack of self-expression (expressing your opinions and feelings)	• Subjugation • Self-sacrifice • Approval seeking
Constrained, short-falling child	Lack of spontaneity, play and relaxation (excessive control)	• Negativity/ pessimism • Emotional inhibition • High demands • Punitiveness
Victimised child	Lack of fairness	• Unfairness/ dishonesty
Confused child	Lack of a coherent picture of yourself and of the world	• Confusion about who you are

Shame) and doesn't belong (Social Isolation/Alienation). Your pitfalls are always present in the background, and when you revert to a vulnerable child mode because of a certain event, this determines your feelings, thoughts and behaviour.

Vulnerable child modes as a result of resignation to pitfalls (unfulfilled basic needs)

Little Martin experienced a lack of autonomy and was not allowed to express his feelings and opinions (pitfalls of Dependence/Incompetence and Failure), which led to the dependent, failing Martin.

Almost none of **little Nora's** basic needs were adequately met, and she experienced especially serious deficits in the areas of acceptance, connection, security and predictability (pitfalls of Mistrust/Abuse, Abandonment/Instability, Social Isolation/Alienation, Emotional Deprivation, Defectiveness/ Shame). This led to abandoned, abused, disregarded Nora.

Little Sarah had a lack of attention to her feelings and too little space for spontaneity and play (pitfalls of High Demands and Emotional Inhibition), leading to constrained, deficient Sarah.

These are of course just a few examples. Which of your basic needs were not adequately met? Use Tables 2.1 and 2.2 to help you think about this.

This means that when you enter a vulnerable child mode, you are usually overwhelmed by intense feelings, similar to a (small) child's reactions to a threat, abandonment, neglect, limitation or unfairness. Children usually become very anxious or sad in such cases. This is very normal when you're still young and haven't learnt to deal with things like this yet, but for an adult, these reactions are far too violent – even if they're understandable if you didn't learn from your parents to attune your emotions to what is going on and to resolve difficult situations. You have developed virtually no healthy adult mode (see p. 58), and you therefore behave like a young child who can't handle their emotions very well yet.

If you want to describe what your vulnerable child mode looks like, read the 'Explanation of the modes' download, which elaborates on the different modes, and complete the 'My vulnerable child mode' worksheet from *Breaking Negative Thinking Patterns*. You can also use this to identify which basic need was not met, and what is needed now. (Both files can be found at https://www. wiley.com/go/breakingnegativepatterns/1e.)

Angry child modes

Irritation and anger are normal reactions to unpleasant situations in which your needs are not being met. Getting angry when you feel someone is treating you badly gives you the space to release your tension and the power to change something about the situation. But if you express your anger too violently or in an indirect way, you are in one of the angry child modes.

The angry child mode (the 'angry child' for short) becomes active when you feel that your needs are not adequately being considered (again). You also give this mode its own name, for example 'angry [your name]' or 'defiant [your name]'. Angry child mode is a collective term for all kinds of angry reactions. For the sake of convenience, we refer to all forms of anger described below as the angry child, but remember that the angry child can express itself in different ways. For example, someone might express irritation as anger or rage, but it may also take the form of rebellious behaviour or sulking. Note that not all forms of angry behaviour mean that the angry child is active. Angry behaviour can also stem from a coping mode, for example becoming cynical and angry as an avoidant coping mode (see p. 45), attacking and being arrogant as an inversion coping mode (see p. 50), or a healthy (controlled) angry reaction from the healthy adult (see Exercise 7.1, p. 215). With the angry child, this always involves uncontrolled anger.

This is not that specific to a specific need, but can occur when one or more basic needs are not met (see Table 2.3). Your concrete reaction depends on both the situation in which you feel one of your needs is not being respected and on your temperament. There are people with a short fuse, who react angrily, or even furiously, when hurt (like Nora). The angry or enraged child can

Table 2.3 Angry child modes

Mode	Deficits	Potential pitfalls
Angry child	Can occur in all forms of deficiency	• Can occur with any pitfall
Sulking child	Lack of autonomy, competence and identity	• Enmeshment/ entanglement
	Lack of realistic limits and self-control	• Lack of self-discipline and self-control
	Lack of spontaneity, play and relaxation (excessive control)	• High demands • Punitiveness
Rebellious child	Lack of autonomy, competence and identity	• Enmeshment/ entanglement
	Lack of self-expression (expressing your opinions and feelings)	• Subjugation
	Lack of spontaneity, play and relaxation (excessive control)	• High demands • Punitiveness
Enraged child	Can occur with all forms of deficits, but especially with a lack of boundaries and self-control	• Entitlement (grandiosity)

then scream, break things or even attack people. Someone with a somewhat restrained temperament can also express anger indirectly. For example, a person deliberately does not do what is expected of him or her (rebellious or passive-aggressive behaviour), stubbornly does not do something or does it only with great reluctance (sulking). The sulking child is often a reaction to excessive interference, or high demands placed on them, by others. The defiant or rebellious child usually rebels against others having a restrictive or authoritarian attitude.

As with the vulnerable child mode, the last column of the table shows which pitfalls you might have for each angry child mode as a result of specific deficits. Again, this does not mean that if you are in defiant child mode, for example you have all four of these pitfalls – but you might have more than one. In that mode, one person might rebel against Subjugation and another against High Demands. Your pitfalls are always present in the background, and when you get into to an angry child mode because of a certain event, this determines your thoughts, feelings and behaviour.

If you want to describe what your angry child mode looks like, read the 'Explanation of the modes' download and complete the 'My angry child mode' worksheet from *Breaking Negative Thinking Patterns*. You can also use this to identify which basic need was not met and what is needed now. (Both files can be found at https://www.wiley.com/go/breakingnegativepatterns/1e.)

There are also people who are angry inside, but do not express it at all and bottle up their feelings. Among other things, this can lead to feelings of depression or misunderstood physical symptoms (as in Martin's case). For a detailed explanation of this, see the section 'Learning to express your anger in balance' in Chapter 6 (p. 185). Treatment with schema therapy is intended to teach you to express your anger in a healthy way (see steps 3 and 4 in Chapters 5 and 6).

Impulsive, undisciplined and spoilt child modes

Vulnerable child mode and angry child mode are the most common child modes, but some people also have impulsive, undisciplined or spoilt child mode. Again, you combine these modes with your own name: 'impulsive/undisciplined/spoilt [your name]'. Although these child modes are less common, it is important to understand and recognise them. They do require a different approach (see Chapter 6 for more on this).

For example, you are in an impulsive child mode if you react impulsively when one of your basic needs is not met. This can happen with many pitfalls (see Table 2.4). For example, if you're afraid of being let down, you might start compulsively checking on the other person or do other impulsive things to prevent someone from letting you down. And if you feel lonely, left out or emotionally neglected, the impulsive child mode could lead you to enter into new (short-term) relationships without thinking, just to feel less alone for a while. Impulsively seeking advice, reassurance or help from others stems from Dependence/Incompetence, the feeling of not being able to do anything or from Vulnerability to Harm and Illness. You might also impulsively attract attention, believing you have a special right to the attention, recognition or even admiration of others.

A second type of mode is the undisciplined child. You have not developed sufficient self-control, and if you do not feel motivated to do boring or difficult tasks, you are easily distracted and impulsively go have fun. This might get you into trouble in the long run. Finally, there is the spoilt child mode. With the idea that you are special, you impose your will to force instant gratification of your needs and you boast about who you are and what you can do.

Table 2.4 Impulsive, undisciplined and spoilt child modes

Mode	Deficits	Potential pitfalls
Impulsive child	Lack of acceptance, connection, security and predictability	• Mistrust/abuse • Abandonment/instability • Social isolation/alienation • Emotional deprivation • Defectiveness/shame
	Lack of autonomy, competence and identity	• Dependence/incompetence • Vulnerability to harm and illness
	Lack of self-expression (expressing your opinions and feelings)	• Approval seeking
	Lack of realistic limits and self-control	• Entitlement (grandiosity) • Lack of self-discipline and self-control
	Lack of spontaneity, play and relaxation	• Punitiveness
	Lack of fairness	• Unfairness/dishonesty
Undisciplined child	Lack of realistic limits and self-control	• Lack of self-discipline and self-control
Spoilt child	Lack of realistic limits and self-control	• Entitlement (grandiosity)

The last column again shows what pitfalls you might have as a result of specific deficits in each kind of child mode. Again, this doesn't mean you have all these pitfalls if you are in a particular child mode – but you may have more than one. In that mode, one person might react impulsively to Abandonment/Instability and another to Punitiveness. Your pitfalls are always present in the background, and if you revert to an impulsive, undisciplined, spoilt child mode because of a certain event, this determines your feelings, thoughts and behaviour.

If you want to describe what your impulsive, undisciplined, grandiose spoilt child mode looks like, read the 'Explanation of the modes' download and complete the 'My impulsive, undisciplined or spoiled child mode' worksheet from *Breaking Negative Thinking Patterns*. You can also use this to identify which basic need was not met and what is needed now. (Both files can be found at https://www.wiley.com/go/breakingnegativepatterns/1e.)

Critical modes

When you think very negatively about yourself, one of your critical modes is active. For example, you think you are stupid, ugly, lazy or self-centred. You exclusively focus on the negative things about yourself. At the same time, you are convinced that others see you the same way. That leads you to assume that they are disappointed in you, would rather not interact with you and are likely to laugh at you, judge you, punish you or even abuse you – all of which is your own fault. If you have a critical mode, you either surrender to the pitfall of Punitiveness or to the pitfalls of High Demands and Emotional Inhibition (see Table 2.5).

If you are in a critical mode, usually you don't even realise yourself that you are thinking so negatively about yourself.

Table 2.5 Critical modes

Mode	Deficits	Potential pitfalls
Demanding mode	Lack of spontaneity, play and relaxation (excessive control)	• Emotional inhibition • High demands
Punitive mode	Lack of spontaneity, play and relaxation (excessive control)	• Punitiveness
Guilt-inducing mode	Lack of spontaneity, play and relaxation (excessive control)	• Punitiveness
	Lack of self-expression (expressing your opinions and feelings)	• Subjugation

You often experience your thoughts as normal. Some people who are in this mode literally hear a voice criticising them.

Critical modes are sometimes also called parent modes because it is often negative messages from your parents that have led you to consider yourself bad, stupid, ugly, etc. (punitive mode), think everything is your fault or that you are selfish (blaming mode) or think you are a failure and think you should try harder (demanding mode). Apart from the messages or examples set by your parents or others, critical modes can also be caused by what peers (bullies) or other important people from your childhood said to you.

You do not give critical modes your own name because they represent the negative messages from others in your past that have gotten under your skin. Children tend to believe what is said about them. If they are treated badly, ignored or neglected, they usually think it is their fault. You are not born with these negative views of yourself. It is therefore important to describe the messages from the critical modes in the 'you' form. So you don't phrase what they tell you as '*I* am stupid and ugly', but as '*You* are stupid and ugly'.

The critical modes and the child modes often occur together. If, from the punitive mode, you think 'You are stupid and lazy', you are almost immediately overwhelmed by a powerless, dejected and anxious feeling (the abandoned, abused, disregarded child). I explain the critical modes in more detail here.

Demanding mode

If you are in the demanding mode, you are setting the bar far too high and you do not have healthy ambition. You force yourself to do everything perfectly and think you have to finish all your tasks before you can allow yourself any relaxation. You don't really want to waste time on 'useless' things like play and fun. And idleness is completely out of the question. This critical mode primarily relates to work, school or other domains where the focus is on performance. Sometimes it also places excessive demands on your appearance or health.

Typical statements from the demanding mode are:

- Until you've done it perfectly, it's no good.
- You always have to be the best.
- You have to keep going until it is finished or perfect.
- You have to do everything to stay slim or healthy.
- Resting or doing something fun when you aren't finished is lazy.
- It could always be better.

This mode develops in your childhood because your parents, teachers or sports coaches always emphasised performance and weren't interested in anything else. Doing things for fun is a waste of time. Performing normally and getting average grades is not good enough. If you're a good student, then only top marks are acceptable. Or maybe you're not a very good student, but quite creative, musical or athletic, but that is not seen as a valuable trait. *Unless*, perhaps, you are actually particularly outstanding in that. Then, in that field, you are driven to deliver ever-greater achievements. With that, all the enjoyment you might have in those activities is lost. Your value is measured solely by your performance and not by who you are as a person. You exhaust yourself emotionally and physically, and with that you are heading for burnout.

Some parents or caregivers are not very aware of the pressure they put on their children. Perhaps they actually only indirectly show that performance is ultimately the only thing that counts. Maybe they never literally said they didn't like or love you if you got a 6 or 7 out of 10 on a test, but gave you that message indirectly, for instance by comparing you to a sibling who did better than you. Or they only complimented you on high grades, but never on average performance or things not necessarily related to achievement. Or even more subtly: they invariably reacted with disappointment if one time you didn't win at football. It is also possible that they set an example of performance pressure in their own lives by always working hard themselves and never making time for relaxation or fun.

Sarah was mainly influenced by the example her parents always set for her. Both worked incredibly hard, and they didn't pay much attention to her feelings. This has led to a demanding side to her personality.

If you want to describe what your demanding mode looks like, read the 'Explanation of the modes' download and complete the 'My demanding mode' worksheet from *Breaking Negative Thinking Patterns*. You can also use this to identify which basic need was not met and what is needed now. (Both files can be found at https://www.wiley.com/go/breakingnegativepatterns/1e.)

The demanding mode often occurs in combination with the dependent, failing or constrained short-falling child mode and is often accompanied by feelings of melancholy, stress and anxiety. If you don't make it to the top, you're a loser. This leads to dejection and puts you at risk of exhaustion, and sometimes it also manifests itself in negative behaviour against other people who are not trying as hard as you are. A possible consequence of an overactive demanding mode is not only that you become exhausted, but also that you neglect or even lose your friends and family.

What is healthy ambition?

We live in a time when there is a focus on performance in many areas. Not only at work, but also in your private life. Being a good employee is not enough, you have to get a promotion. You should not only be a good partner, but also a perfect parent to your children. You are also expected to engage in many social activities and don't forget to exercise every day. The trick is not to overdo it. There is nothing at all wrong with wanting to achieve something and doing your best. But don't do that at all costs. Remain realistic about what can fit into a 24-hour day. The most important thing is that you enjoy your activities and have time for relaxation.

If the emphasis is actually always on performing in almost all areas of your life, you have to watch out. You really don't need to be afraid that you'll never get anything done if you take time off once in a while and do something purely for fun. Your healthy adult mode is perfectly capable of balancing performance and responsibilities on one hand with fun and relaxation on the other.

Punitive mode

If you have a strong punitive mode, you reject yourself and feel ashamed of yourself. That negative judgement usually relates to your whole person or your whole life. You not only think you're doing it wrong (as in the demanding mode), but believe you are wrong. You see yourself as bad, worthless, stupid and unattractive. You fear that other people will reject you if they really get to know you. That they will abandon you or take advantage of you. When push comes to shove, you're on your own. You don't really belong anyway, and you're a bad person. Because of that, you deserve punishment for everything that goes wrong, and if misfortune befalls you, you deserve it.

Typical statements of the punitive mode are:

- You are bad, stupid and ugly.
- You should never have been born.
- If something goes wrong, it is your own fault.
- If something goes wrong or goes against you, don't complain.
- No one actually wants anything to do with you.

A punitive mode is usually created by quite severe rejection by your parents or others, such as bullies at school. There was a continuous lack of safety and security in different areas and a lack of emotional support. We will review these causes in brief.

A lack of safety is a first major potential factor in the origin of the punitive mode. That lack of safety may be related to sexual and/or physical abuse and psychological abuse.

Sexual assault often takes place in the domestic environment, but sometimes also by other people you should really be able to trust, such as a teacher or a coach. Sexual abuse often occurs in secret. The perpetrator threatens you as a child with terrible consequences for you or your family if it comes out. He (sometimes she) also tries to make you believe it is actually your own fault that this is happening. This often makes children afraid to talk about it because they are scared and feel guilty. This makes you more vulnerable to abuse later in life because you think you don't deserve better.

Physical abuse usually takes place at home, but sometimes it is other children who abuse you, for example when there is no parental supervision. These could be siblings or bullies at school. People who abuse children usually lack self-control, but sometimes they are also sadistic and take pleasure in harming others. Fear and powerlessness as a child can mean that you don't dare to tell anyone. Physical abuse includes physical assault (hitting, kicking or burning) and extreme punishment, such as being put outside naked, locked in a dark cellar or denied food. Being poorly cared for, such as not getting enough food or not having clean clothes, can also cause a lasting sense of insecurity.

Psychological abuse can cause as much damage as physical abuse. Being constantly scolded and humiliated, or excluded by caregivers or peers, can lead to the feeling of being alone in the world. Maybe your parents were often not at home when you were very small. Or you didn't get attention for your emotions and were made out to be exaggerating, or ignored, when you experienced something unpleasant. This is all very painful. Bullies can also do a lot of emotional damage by calling you names or breaking your belongings. Especially if the bullies are at your school, it is almost impossible to escape from them, and they can target you for years. Parents often don't know what to do about it or say you should 'just hit back'. Saying that just makes it worse.

Another factor is if one of your parents leaves the family or if a parent dies, and you do not receive sufficient explanation, care and consolation. Then, as a child, you might start thinking that your father or mother didn't think it was worth staying with you. Or the other parent breaks down after losing their partner and can no longer care for you. This can also lead to a punitive mode: in a child, it may evoke the belief that they are not important enough to deserve care. It's not just about negative things said directly to you, but also indirect messages. If you don't get care or attention, then as a child you conclude yourself that you are obviously not worthwhile and have no reason to exist.

All these kinds of experiences can trigger a strong sense of defectiveness, the feeling that no one loves you, you are alone in the world and you can't trust anyone. This lack of trust is also directed at care providers and makes accepting help more complicated, as we will see with Nora in particular.

If you want to describe what your punitive mode looks like, read the 'Explanation of the modes' download and complete the 'My punitive mode' worksheet from *Breaking Negative Thinking Patterns*. You can also use this to identify which basic need was not met and what is needed now. (Both files can be found at https://www.wiley.com/go/breakingnegativepatterns/1e.)

Guilt-inducing mode

In this mode, you feel guilty towards others too easily. You think you don't care for others enough. You constantly feel responsible for their well-being and are always available to them. You are very understanding of others and remain kind and caring to everyone, even if they don't treat you very well. Without realising it yourself, you regularly overstep your own boundaries in the process.

Typical statements of the blaming mode are:

- You should always be there for everyone.
- It is your fault if your family or friends are not happy.
- Putting your needs first is egoistic.
- If others have difficulties, it is your duty to resolve that.

If one or both parent(s) were often mentally or physically ill in your childhood or if a sibling needed extra care, you may start to feel responsible for others far too early. That feeling is compounded when one parent is having problems and the other just can't handle everything very well. Moreover, it is not unusual in this kind of situation that the parents do not organise or accept outside help, so the pressure on the family to solve it themselves, and with that the pressure on you as a child, is particularly high. As a child, you then take over your parents' caregiving responsibilities of your own accord, even if you are far too young to do that. Once you're in such a situation as a child, you are likely to find that nothing you do is enough to make others happy. This drives you to labour harder and harder for others – after all, you are responsible for their well-being.

If you also sense that they can't handle having your big and small worries added to it, they further teach you that your needs and your opinions don't matter, and that it's better to keep them to yourself. And precisely because you seem so strong, there is much too little care and attention for you because you are seen as the child who can handle everything. You think others undoubtedly have it much harder than you. In many cases, parents are actually not very aware that they are giving their child a feeling of guilt. They probably only indirectly signal that their son or daughter should always take care of others and adapt to their needs.

In Martin's case, for instance, the blaming mode was primarily caused by the example set by his mother who always just went along with what his father wanted. There, the feeling arose that he had to help his mother with the household because she had so many concerns about his sick sister and couldn't easily handle the household on her own.

In some families, it is even dangerous for children not to adapt to the situation at home. In that case, for example (the threat of) aggression by the parents plays a role. Especially if the other parent cannot stand up to that aggression, and always just tries to appease the aggressor, you automatically learn that it is better to keep quiet about your needs and your opinion. This kind of parent is a role model who teaches you that it is wiser always just to adapt. You unconsciously start taking care of that 'weaker' parent to try to make him or her happy. Of course, that is doomed to fail, but as a child this always leaves you feeling guilty.

If you want to describe what your blaming mode looks like, read the 'Explanation of the modes' download and complete the 'My blaming mode' worksheet from *Breaking Negative Thinking Patterns*. You can also use this to identify which basic need was not met and what is needed now. (Both files can be found at https://www.wiley.com/go/breakingnegativepatterns/1e.)

Coping modes

The coping style of *resignation* to your pitfalls can lead to the unhelpful child modes and critical modes described above. The coping styles *avoidance* and *inversion* lead to the avoidant and inversion coping modes, respectively. They are sometimes also called 'protectors': you protect yourself from too much emotional pain such as fear, sadness or anger. What these modes have in common is that they prevent you from feeling that one or more of your basic needs are not being met. In your childhood, these modes were more or less 'protectors' because they made sure you didn't suffer too much from the unhealthy circumstances you grew up in. In your present life, they are no longer functional as protectors, as will be explained below.

Avoidance can lead to eight types of modes and inversion even up to 12 (see below). That seems like a lot, but you probably only have two or three of them yourself. After all, everyone has different pitfalls and therefore different ways of minimising their effect. Investigate which method(s) of avoidance and/or inversion suit you best, based on your main pitfalls.

You developed these coping modes in childhood as emergency solutions to cope with difficult situations. They seem helpful at first because, with them, you don't feel as bad when you fall into a pitfall and risk being overwhelmed by the negative feelings and thoughts caused by the child modes and critical modes. These coping modes can become automatic, and you carry them with you to this day. In your present life, they still protect you from the messages of your critical modes and being overwhelmed by the unpleasant feelings of the child modes, just like before. Even so, this does not really benefit you anymore in your adult life. Indeed, these strategies stand in the way of healthy development. They are rigid and extreme, you do not adequately understand what you actually need in order to fulfil your basic needs, and you don't learn to deal with your feelings constructively. Furthermore, they create distance between you and other people, even when that is not necessary.

When you encounter an unpleasant situation in your current life that reminds you of the past, you often automatically react in a way that is familiar to you. Your emotional bruise is in danger of being hurt again, and you don't want to feel that pain. First of all, you can do that by avoiding unpleasant feelings in a painful or threatening situation. You shut off your feelings, numb them, make extreme adjustments or literally just avoid situations. The other way to avoid suffering from negative thoughts and feelings is to turn things around. This then involves inversion or overcompensation. You then behave as if the opposite of your pitfall is true. Instead, you pretend you can handle anything and you feel great, by playing the clown, acting as if you're better than others, or acting like you don't need anyone. You can try to do everything perfectly or, on the contrary, pretend that performance is totally unimportant. If that doesn't help enough, you can also go on the attack (because offence is still the best defence), manipulate people or behave recklessly.

Note: everyone has coping modes for difficult situations! They can actually help to some extent if a situation is too difficult or dangerous for you. But if you stay in a coping mode for too long, when the difficult situation is already behind you, it becomes a problem. Suppose you switched off your feelings a little bit when you were faced with an angry colleague at work. If you stay stuck in that mode afterwards and continue to react absently or numbly, for example when you're already back home, your coping style is no longer functional. Also, if you apply a mode too readily, it hinders you more than it helps you move forward. Sarah always prepares her lessons very well and always checks the students' work very carefully because she feels that she does have to deliver quality at the college. To some extent, that is actually appropriate to her position. But she puts so much energy into her work (demanding mode) that she has no time for normal relaxation, so her Detached Self-Soother coping mode automatically kicks in as soon as she gets home. In her case, that consists of spending hours on the computer or watching TV series and neglecting her relationships and friendships.

I will now describe the different forms of avoidance and inversion. See if you recognise yourself in one or more types. Maybe you use different coping modes in different situations, or you always use the same strategy everywhere. Think back to a moment when you fell into a coping mode and consider whether a child mode or a critical mode was active just before that. Also try to discover how or from whom you learnt these coping modes in your childhood.

Avoidant coping mode

Your avoidant coping mode consists of various ways to reduce, numb or avoid feelings when your critical mode is too hard on you or when you risk being overwhelmed by negative feelings from your child mode. You can avoid conflict or negative behaviour from others, as well as negative feelings or thoughts about yourself. The avoidant coping modes described below can occur separately or in combination with each other. In fact, you can use all of them to avoid feeling deficits in your upbringing. Table 2.6 shows which avoidant coping modes commonly occur with which deficits.

The detached protector (shutting off feelings). You can shut off your feelings in different ways. You can try not to think about something or ignore your feelings. Some people can shut off their feelings by turning within themselves when surrounded by others and not reacting to anything. In extreme cases, it can even lead to you really not noticing anything going on around you. This is also called dissociation. Other people use substances such as alcohol, hashish or sedatives to subdue their feelings.

The funny protector (making jokes). When someone says something hurtful, you respond with a funny remark. That makes it seem as if you don't care when someone says something unpleasant to you, and you take it as funny.

The angry protector (becoming cynical or angry). You can also make cynical jokes or even become angry as a defence against people who cause you pain. Instead of saying that something is annoying or painful to you, you either ridicule the other person or return any criticism with the same venom.

Table 2.6 Avoidant coping mode

Method of avoidance	Deficits	Pitfalls
The Detached Protector (shutting off feelings)	With virtually all deficits, except lack of boundaries and self-control	• All pitfalls, except: • Entitlement (grandiosity) • Lack of self-discipline and self-control
The Funny Protector (making jokes)	Lack of acceptance, connection, security and predictability Lack of autonomy, competence and identity Lack of self-expression (expressing your opinions and feelings)	• Mistrust/abuse • Abandonment/instability • Social isolation/alienation • Emotional deprivation • Defectiveness/shame • Dependence/incompetence • Failure • Vulnerability to harm and illness • Enmeshment/entanglement • Subjugation
The Angry Protector (becoming cynical or angry)	Lack of acceptance, connection, security and predictability Lack of spontaneity, play and relaxation (excessive control)	• Mistrust/abuse • Social isolation/alienation • Defectiveness/shame • Emotional inhibition
The Avoidant Protector (avoiding situations)	With virtually all deficits	• All pitfalls

The Detached Self-soother (seeking distraction)	With virtually all deficits	• All pitfalls except Subjugation
The Compliant Surrenderer (the Subordinate)	Lack of acceptance, connection, security and predictability Lack of autonomy, competence and identity Lack of self-expression (expressing your opinions and feelings)	• Abandonment/instability • Emotional deprivation • Dependence/incompetence • Enmeshment/entanglement • Subjugation
The Reassurance Seeker	Lack of acceptance, connection, security and predictability Lack of autonomy, competence and identity	• Abandonment/instability • Dependence/incompetence • Failure • Vulnerability to harm and illness
The Suspicious Overcontroller (paranoid need for control)	Lack of acceptance, connection, security and predictability	• Mistrust and abuse • Abandonment/instability

The avoidant protector (avoiding situations). You can avoid your feelings by literally not going somewhere because you're afraid of encountering unpleasant people there or because you feel awkward. You may also shy away from difficult conversations with others while there is something bothering you. Finally, you can refuse tasks you dread or not try new things at work or in your free time.

The detached self-soother (seeking distraction). You can also numb unpleasant feelings by actively seeking distractions, such as working much too hard, exercising too much, watching movies for hours, surfing the internet or playing computer games. It can also take the form of compulsively watching porn or gambling. Of course, many of these activities are also just relaxing, but if you do them too often and for too long, when you should actually be doing something else, it becomes a problem.

The compliant surrenderer (the subordinate). Always doing what others expect of you and being there for them will at least prevent you from being criticised or running into a conflict. You adopt the preferences of others and stop considering what your own needs are or where your boundaries lie. You don't dare to chart your own path. In extreme situations, you accept being treated badly or being taken advantage of in various ways.

The reassurance seeker. If you are worried about your health or your relationships with other people, it helps to seek reassurance by asking if your worries are justified. But if you keep asking others if nothing is wrong, even if they have already assured you extensively that everything is fine, this can also be a way of avoiding your fears and insecurities rather than enduring or processing them. Endless complaining and moaning about relatively insignificant inconveniences or unpleasant events can also have this function.

The suspicious overcontroller (paranoid need for control). If you feel that you can't trust anyone and you're afraid that others will exploit you or let you down, you can avoid that by constantly keeping an eye on everyone. You believe you continually have to defend yourself against attacks, abandonment or cheating. You can only achieve this by blaming others, keeping tabs on them and always being alert to conspiracies.

Avoidant coping modes

Sarah has the avoidant coping mode *Detached Self-Soother*. She works much too hard and watches a lot of TV series or looks at the internet for hours in her spare time.

Martin has the avoidant coping mode *Compliant Surrenderer* (the Subordinate). He adapts to accommodate family, friends and colleagues and takes on tasks he doesn't really have time for.

Nora has the avoidant coping mode *Detached Protector*. She does everything on autopilot and, in the company of others, does not react when something happens that affects her.

If you want to describe what your avoidant mode looks like, read the 'Explanation of the modes' download and complete the 'My avoidant mode' worksheet from *Breaking Negative Thinking Patterns*. You can also use this to identify which basic need was not met and what is needed now. (Both files can be found at https://www.wiley.com/go/breakingnegativepatterns/1e.)

Inversion coping mode

Another way of not thinking about what you need and escaping unpleasant feelings is to act in the opposite way to how you really feel inside. This is called the inversion coping mode. It often comes down to 'shouting yourself down', but it can actually also lead to overly nice and modest or lazy behaviour. For example, if you actually feel very dependent, you act as if you don't need anyone. Or if you're insecure, you act as if you've really got it made. Or if you set very high standards for yourself, you act very lazy. At first glance, these approaches to inversion might resemble healthy behaviour. Isn't it good to be independent, have self-confidence and not come across as excessively ambitious? Sometimes a little inversion is not a problem at all when you're in a difficult situation. Here, this is more about one-sided and extreme expressions of inversion, which become irritating and tiresome for you or others. See if you recognise yourself in one or more types. Maybe you sometimes use an avoidant mode and other times an inversion coping mode. Think back to a moment when you fell into an inversion coping mode and consider whether a child mode or critical mode was active just before that. Also try to discover how you learnt this coping mode in your childhood, or from whom.

I describe several inversion coping modes here. They can occur separately or in combination with each other. With most inversion coping modes, you are the main one to suffer. The last three (Self-aggrandiser, Attacker and Deceiver) are more irritating or harmful to others. Table 2.7 shows which inversion commonly occurs with which deficits.

Table 2.7 Inversion coping modes

Method of inversion	Deficits	Pitfalls
The hyper autonomous/ independent	Lack of acceptance, connection, security and predictability	• Abandonment/instability
	Lack of autonomy, competence and identity	• Dependence/incompetence
	Lack of self-expression (expressing your opinions and feelings)	• Enmeshment/entanglement • Subjugation • Self-sacrifice • Approval
The clown	Lack of acceptance, connection, security and predictability	• Mistrust/abuse • Abandonment/instability • Emotional deprivation • Social isolation/alienation • Defectiveness/shame
	Lack of autonomy, competence and identity	• Dependence/incompetence • Failure • Vulnerability to harm and illness • Enmeshment/entanglement
	Lack of self-expression (expressing your opinions and feelings)	• Subjugation • Self-sacrifice
	Lack of spontaneity, play and relaxation (excessive control)	• Negativity/pessimism • Emotional inhibition

(*Continued*)

Table 2.7 (Continued)

Method of inversion	Deficits	Pitfalls
The attention-and approval seeker	Lack of acceptance, connection, security and predictability Lack of spontaneity, play and relaxation (excessive control)	• Emotional deprivation • Defectiveness/shame • Social isolation/alienation • Emotional inhibition
The daredevil	Lack of autonomy, competence and identity	• Vulnerability to harm and illness
The perfectionistic overcontroller	Lack of acceptance, connection, security and predictability Lack of autonomy, competence and identity Lack of realistic limits and self-control	• Emotional deprivation • Failure • Lack of self-discipline and self-control
The slacker/oblomov	Lack of spontaneity, play and relaxation (excessive control)	• High demands
The over-optimist/pollyanna	Lack of spontaneity, play and relaxation (excessive control) Lack of fairness	• Negativity/pessimism • Unfairness/dishonesty
The saint (the over humble)	Lack of spontaneity, play and relaxation (excessive control) Lack of realistic limits and self-control	• Punitiveness • Entitlement (grandiosity)

The self-aggrandiser	Lack of acceptance, connection, security and predictability Lack of self-expression (expressing your opinions and feelings)	• Defectiveness/shame • Social isolation/alienation • Subjugation • Self-sacrifice • Approval
The bully and attacker	Lack of acceptance, connection, security and predictability Lack of self-expression (expressing your opinions and feelings) Lack of fairness	• Mistrust/abuse • Abandonment/instability • Subjugation • Unfairness/dishonesty
The manipulator and cheater	Lack of acceptance, connection, security and predictability Lack of fairness	• Abandonment/instability • Unfairness/dishonesty

The hyper-autonomous/independent. You don't need anyone and also prefer not to ask others for advice because that is weak. You also don't want a long-term relationship and act as if you're happy single. But deep down, you are actually afraid that you might be let down by your partner or friends. You're also often afraid that others will put too much pressure on you or force you into things you don't want. If you don't allow others into your life, they can't hurt you.

The clown. You ridicule any indication that you have certain needs. Whether it is a desire for security, stability or autonomy, the clown mocks it. All those needs and feelings are soft, childish, absurd or exaggerated, so you don't need to worry about them, or you make (inappropriate) jokes about them.

The attention-and-approval seeker. If you don't want to acknowledge that you feel defective and disregarded, or are afraid of not fitting in, you can ward off those feelings by making yourself the centre of everything. You try to gain approval and recognition from others by telling interesting stories about what you can do or have experienced. This superficial contact replaces the love or attention you really need. Paradoxically, however, this is exactly what you don't get because the attention-getter will eventually irritate people.

The daredevil. Are you very afraid of getting sick or things going wrong in your life, but don't want to seek reassurance from others all the time? You can then suppress or ignore your fear by actually seeking out the danger. 'The Daredevil' ridicules real risks.

The perfectionistic overcontroller. Do you often feel like a loser, struggle with self-control and self-discipline, or perhaps you're used to only getting attention when you perform well? In that case, exhibiting the opposite behaviour, by furiously trying your best and making as few mistakes as possible, is your coping style to avoid feeling failed or lonely.

A variation of this is that you compete with everyone about who is the best, so you constantly get confirmation that you are better than your 'opponent'.

The slacker/oblomov. Have you been a perfectionist since childhood because your educators mainly emphasised performance, but found that it was still never good enough? As a counter-reaction, you can actually stop making any demands on yourself at all and elevate idleness and doing nothing to an art form.

The over-optimist/pollyanna. If you are pessimistic or see injustice and abuse everywhere, sometimes it becomes so intolerable that you prefer to close your eyes to it. You start acting overly optimistic and believe that everyone has good intentions, even when there is no reason to think so. While there is nothing wrong with basic trust in people or hoping for a happy outcome if you have problems, it is important to maintain a somewhat realistic view of people and situations.

The saint (the over humble). If you are very humble or modest, it seems very likeable at first. However, if this becomes excessive, it can also prove to be an inversion of the idea that you are actually very special. Extreme modesty sometimes conceals the fear that other people will think you are arrogant if you show that you're good at something.

The self-aggrandiser. You consider yourself to be better, smarter, more skilful and more successful than other people. You brag about who you know and look down on people who are not as lucky. You think you are good to other people, but in reality you take advantage of them if it suits you better. You behave this way to avoid acknowledging that you actually feel inferior and isolated, or afraid that others will domineer over you. Other people often find you arrogant or boastful and may also call you a narcissist.

The bully and attacker. Offence is the best defence – at least according to some people who are afraid of being abandoned, abused, mistreated or subjugated. Perhaps you were traumatised in your childhood to the extent that you no longer trust anyone. By harassing or belittling someone to the point that they don't dare to leave you, or by threatening someone so that they will not cheat or abuse you, you feel dominant and your fear disappears.

If you are afraid of being treated unfairly, you can attack the other person directly, but you can also make plans to target the other person in a calculated way. Like a predator, you hunt your prey. You execute your plans ruthlessly. You may feel safe, but others become afraid of you.

The manipulator and cheater. You can also make yourself feel safe in more subtle ways and prevent others from letting you down or deceiving you. You don't attack them, but spin a web of lies and deceit around them, with which you yourself try to remain invulnerable or untouchable and gain control over the other person.

Inversion coping mode

Sarah's inversion coping mode is 'the Perfectionist'. She always tries her best to do everything as well as possible and competes with others to show who is the best.

Martin's inversion coping mode is 'the Clown'. He acts as if his needs, feelings and opinions are actually ridiculous.

Nora's inversion coping mode is 'the Self-aggrandiser'. She acts tough to avoid showing that she actually feels hurt and then can also act as if she is above everything and everyone else.

If you want to describe what your inversion mode looks like, read the 'Explanation of the modes' download and complete the 'My inversion mode' worksheet from *Breaking Negative Thinking Patterns*. You can also use this to identify which basic need was not met and what is needed now. (Both files can be found at https://www.wiley.com/go/breakingnegativepatterns/1e.)

With this, there are many ways to minimise suffering from not having your basic needs met and not to allow unpleasant feelings, too much self-criticism, excessive demands on yourself or others, or too much guilt. All these coping modes have the same goal: not to feel or think negatively too much. At the same time, they miss the mark because they are so rigid and extreme that they prevent you from acknowledging your basic needs and dealing with emotions in a helpful way. They also cause you to keep others at a distance or even hurt them. Ultimately, with these modes, you precisely do not get what you actually need.

The ultimate goal of schema therapy is therefore to replace these unhelpful modes with a healthy and more flexible posture – which we call the healthy adult mode – and to find a way to feel happy and satisfied – which we describe as the happy child mode. I explain how to achieve that from Chapter 3 onwards.

Helpful modes

Of course, you also learnt things in your childhood that do help you handle life. These healthy modes allow you to handle your emotions, have nuanced thoughts about yourself and develop functioning coping styles. This enables you to organise your life well, overcome setbacks and build good relationships with others. Helpful modes exist when your feelings, thoughts and actions are balanced. This is about the healthy adult mode and the happy child mode.

Healthy adult mode

We also refer to the healthy adult mode as 'big [your own name]', who is the captain of your ship, as it were. This is also a kind of car-ing parent within yourself. Someone who is sensible, but also kind and understanding. Someone who keeps all aspects of life reason-ably in balance. With that, you don't need any unhelpful coping modes from your past because you can just *live* instead of *survive*.

If you are faced with a problem, you know what you can do to solve it. You know who to ask for help without making yourself completely dependent on the advice of others. You sense who you can trust and who you'd better keep your distance from. You are mindful of your own needs and those of others and try to balance them. You have little or no trouble with an overly critical voice in the back of your mind, but can handle criticism and acknowledge your mistakes when necessary. You fulfil your obligations and perform your tasks competently, but also make time for relaxation and fun. Your emotions align well with what is going on: when something nice happens you feel happy and content, and when you face a setback you feel sad, angry or anxious. But you maintain your balance! If you have a minor conflict with a colleague, or someone does something wrong, you won't immediately be furious, but you might be irritated. And if you really have to, you can also get very angry without losing control of yourself.

The 'Explanation of modes' download describes how the healthy adult mode responds when your basic needs are sufficiently met.

Happy child mode

You don't just need a healthy adult mode that enables you to handle the serious things in life but also one that enables you to have fun, relaxation and enjoyment without worries. You got that to a greater or lesser extent in your childhood as well. This carefree and happy side is called the happy child mode or the happy child. It is sometimes also referred to as the free child or the joyful child. Usually, you also give this mode your own name: 'happy [your own name]'. A happy child is the opposite of the hurt, angry or impulsive child and is a good remedy against a critical mode.

You are in your happy child mode when you do things you enjoy. You feel relaxed or have fun. You can fully abandon yourself to enjoyment. What you enjoy is different for everyone. Maybe you like to play sports, sing or garden or go to the theatre, restaurants or dance parties. Playing games with your friends or playing with children is also good for the happy child in you. You feel comfortable, confident and connected with yourself and others. You don't have to perform or prove anything and don't even have to be good at what you are doing – as long as you enjoy it.

If you have a well-developed happy child mode, you usually also have a strong healthy adult mode, which knows when it is time to tackle something seriously and when you can relax.

Summary

If one or more *basic needs* are poorly met in your childhood to a greater or lesser extent, chances are you will develop pitfalls that can affect you throughout your life. Basic needs, for example acceptance, safety, autonomy, competence, spontaneity and realistic boundaries, are universal and the same for everyone. The extent to which one or more basic needs are not met determines how severe your problems are and how many pitfalls you develop.

A *pitfall* is a combination of negative feelings and thoughts about yourself, others and the world that constantly play a role in your life.

To protect yourself from pitfalls, you develop *coping styles* (resignation, avoidance and inversion) that were probably understandable and functional in childhood, but no longer help you as an adult. Pitfalls combined with coping styles lead to *unhelpful modes* (the child modes, critical modes and coping modes). A *mode*, or state of mind, is activated in a difficult situation. It is a type of aspect of your personality that comes very much to the fore, a pattern of feelings, thoughts and behaviour, which disappears again once the difficult situation is over.

The *resignation coping style* leads to the unhelpful *child modes* and *critical modes*: surrendering completely to your pitfalls not only makes you think badly of yourself and gives you an unpleasant feeling, but it also makes you behave accordingly. This is how you develop child modes and critical modes. If one of your *child modes* is activated, you become completely overwhelmed by (negative) emotions and behave like a little sad, angry or impulsive child. The *critical modes* also make you feel bad, but now by constantly pummelling you with negative comments and threatening punishment or a feeling of guilt about who you are and what you do.

The *avoidance coping style* leads to the unhelpful *avoidant coping mode*, where you shut down the negative feelings, thoughts and behaviours caused by your pitfalls or stay away from situations. The downside is that your behaviour makes you avoid all feelings, including the positive ones, and you also stop connecting with the people around you.

The *inversion coping style* leads to the unhelpful *inversion coping mode*, in which you invert the negative thoughts and emotions arising from your pitfall(s): you think the pitfall isn't true and behave in a way that 'proves' the opposite is true. The downside is that this behaviour is often so exaggerated that other people are irritated by you and don't want to have anything to do with you.

None of these modes help you live in a healthy and balanced way. That is why they are also called the unhelpful modes. With this, it is important to develop helpful modes: a *healthy adult mode* and a *happy child mode*. You can do that independently, or by going into schema therapy.

You develop a *healthy adult mode* when all your basic needs are sufficiently met. In most people, this side develops gradually during childhood when their caregivers are attentive and teach them to cope with setbacks in life.

In addition to a healthy adult mode that can handle the serious issues of life, you also have a *happy child mode* that provides plenty of relaxation and fun. You also learn that from your caregivers because they play with you and do other fun things with you.

Schema therapy aims at finally fulfilling your basic needs to develop a stronger healthy adult mode and a happy child mode.

∗∗∗

In the next chapter, you will use different ways to investigate which modes apply to you. This is a necessary first step to discover what you need to work on.

3

Step 1: Discovering your own modes

Do you want to know which modes play a role for you or for others? Do you want to find out where your modes come from? Recognising modes is the first step in the process of change. Describing your modes helps you understand them better, allows you to think about them and helps you be swept away by them less often. Discovering your own modes usually takes four to seven weeks.

Where do you start?

You can discover your modes as follows:

1. Take stock of your current problems.
2. Describe your life history.
3. Fill in questionnaires.
4. Do a visualisation exercise (imagery).
5. Use chairs to get to know modes.

For each part, I describe what Martin, Nora and Sarah did. I also explain what role the therapist or a friend plays in this process.

1. Take stock of your current problems
First of all, make a list of the problems you regularly encounter and consider whether you can already discover certain modes within them. If you are working with a therapist, they will work with you using an example of such a problem to try to find out what you think about the situation, what you feel and what the

underlying belief is that causes you to become upset. Questions that can help with this include: What does this situation mean to you? What do you think others think about that? What is the worst thing that could happen? What does that say about you? It is not always easy to answer those questions because you aren't used to thinking about your problems in this way. Because of this, take time to look for answers and ask your therapist to explain if you aren't very sure.

For example, when Martin tells his therapist that he never protests when he is given an assignment he thinks is way too hard, the therapist discovers that he does this because he's afraid that others will get angry if he refuses. In this way, after some probing, they discover that his idea that it is better always to adapt is a coping mode of his.

A therapist does not usually solve the problem for you, but helps you uncover the connection between your current problem and your modes. At first this can sometimes lead to frustration because you feel that your problems are not being addressed concretely. In other therapies, which specifically target anxiety, depression or an eating disorder, for example you often immediately take the bull by the horns. However, discovering and changing modes takes more time and effort.

You can also ask your partner or friends who know you well if they notice certain patterns of behaviour in you. Especially if you're trying to change your modes on your own, without the help of a therapist, it is a good idea to ask about their perspective. They can also indicate in the subsequent steps if anything about your modes is changing.

Understand that everything you tell your therapist is confidential. Also, ask your friend to keep what you tell her confidential.

Discovering modes in the initial appointments

Martin and **Nora** seek help from a schema therapist to address their pitfalls and to discover their coping styles and modes. Sarah wants to try to change her modes herself. She does confide in a friend who has known her since primary school. She occasionally asks her what she thinks about the steps she is taking and tries to get a clearer picture of her childhood experiences together with her. In response to what someone tells her, the therapist initially only has hypotheses about pitfalls (which she will investigate further using the methods in the following sections).

One of **Sarah's** behavioural patterns is that she works too hard and leaves far too little time to have fun and contact with family and friends. Her friend says she sometimes notices that Sarah sets the bar rather high for herself compared to herself. They examine whether this points to the pitfall of High Demands and the demanding mode.

Martin tells his therapist that he has many physical symptoms such as abdominal pain, headaches and fatigue, but a medical explanation for them has not been found. He complains that he always has to do the unpleasant tasks at work and confesses that he does not know how to deal with this. He does have his roommate as an advisor, but otherwise he has few friends. His therapist notes that one of Martin's modes seems to be that he is quite accommodating to the wishes and opinions of others. His therapist explores with him whether he has the pitfall of Dependence/Incompetence and/or the pitfall of Subjugation and the mode of the dependent, failing child.

Nora tells her therapist that she experiences problems in many areas. She feels that her life has failed and she has many relationship problems. But she still holds back in telling her therapist everything, because she doesn't trust her. She's afraid the therapist will find her too difficult and refer her to someone else. Together, they discuss what causes this distrust and why Nora is so afraid she'll be sent away again. Perhaps Nora has the pitfall of Mistrust/Abuse and/or Abandonment/Instability and the mode of the abandoned, abused child.

2.   Describe your life history

The therapist might ask you to write down the most important facts and events from your childhood. Important questions include:

- What kind of family did you grow up in?
- How did your parents raise you?
- Did unpleasant things happen at home, school or other places?
- How was it handled when you were sad or angry?
- What are the rules of life you took from this?
- Which basic needs were not fulfilled?
- Do you see connections between your past and your current problems?

You can try to gather information about your past through friends and other people who knew you as a child (family, neighbours, teachers, etc.). Objects can also be useful in this process such as photos, videos, letters, diaries or cuddly toys from the past. Our memories are also closely linked to sensory perceptions. It can also help to go back to the place where you lived as a child. Scents or sounds (for example children's songs) can also help you recall memories of the past. The smell of gingerbread can suddenly remind you of that one Christmas Eve and what things were like at home back then. In this way, you can better investigate the connection between your current problems and your own life history. These sources can be especially helpful if you don't remember much of your childhood.

Table 2.1 on page 12 gives an overview of possible deficits in upbringing and the pitfalls that can result. In the following sections, you can explore what coping styles you have and how you developed different modes. Try to find out for yourself if you recognise one or more of these deficits and discuss this with your therapist or a friend. The idea is to talk about your past as openly as possible, even if it is sometimes very painful or you are afraid that you're being too negative about your parents or others. For example, Martin doesn't think his parents did anything wrong. On the contrary, they took very good care of him. Nora especially struggles to talk about the most traumatic situations from her past.

Also read the examples of deficits in how Sarah, Martin and Nora were brought up (p. 15) and consider whether you can already see connections in their situations.

The relationship between life history, unmet basic needs, pitfalls and modes

To some extent, **Sarah** does see a relationship on the one hand between the example her parents set for her by also always working hard and on the other hand the fact that they didn't take her problems seriously and her current problems. She thinks she has experienced a deficit in the area of spontaneity, play and relaxation (pitfalls: High Demands and Emotional Inhibition).

Martin does not really see any connections because he is very happy with his upbringing. His therapist does note that he is very accommodating of others. He explains to Martin that, while it might not be immediately clear what his upbringing has to do with it, he certainly wasn't born with these pitfalls. Somewhere between his birth and now, certain basic needs were not adequately met, influenced by what he experienced in his childhood. There could have been a deficit in autonomy and self-expression (pitfalls: Dependence/Incompetence, Subjugation or Self-sacrifice).

Nora does think there are connections because she experienced a lot of violence and insecurity in her childhood. But she finds it difficult to identify which basic needs were not met and which pitfalls this caused. She is also still afraid to tell everything she has been through. Her therapist thinks Nora felt very unsafe in the past and was lacking in the areas of acceptance, connection, security and predictability (pitfalls: Mistrust/Abuse, Abandonment/Instability and Defectiveness/Shame).

3.   Fill-in questionnaires

You can also use questionnaires to get an idea of your pitfalls and modes. The questionnaires are a relevant, but not the only, source of information to discover your pitfalls. There is a questionnaire that measures pitfalls (the Schema Questionnaire YSQ-S3) and a questionnaire that measures modes (the Schema Mode Inventory SMI). See www.schematherapysociety.com.

Try to answer the questions only for yourself and as honestly as possible. By 'honest', I mean not worrying too much about what others will think of your answers. You decide who gets to see the results. Don't act better than you really feel, but don't act worse either. Your therapist will discuss the outcomes with you and make connections between your current problems and your upbringing. You can also discuss the outcomes with your friend and ask if she recognises them. Your friend can also fill out these questionnaires herself to see what pitfalls and modes she may have.

4.   Do a visualisation exercise (imagery)

A visualisation exercise, also called imagery, is an exercise in which you imagine a particular situation from the past, present or future, and try to put yourself into that situation as well as you can, as if it were happening all over again. The purpose of the exercise is to explore how you felt then and what you thought then in order to find out whether today's pitfalls and modes might be related to that experience. In this first step, you use imagery to explore the connections between your current problems and your upbringing.

How a visualisation exercise works is explained below, for example if you want to try it yourself. You can use the 'Visualisation Exercise Worksheet' (Appendix 4) to do this.

Exercise 3.1

Visualisation exercise to discover pitfalls and modes

1. Select a place where you cannot be disturbed. Sit comfortably and close your eyes. First start by visualising a happy place where you feel comfortable, safe and carefree. Try to imagine really being there and even smelling the smells and seeing the colours associated with that place and hearing the sounds. Are you alone? Or are you with someone, or maybe an animal? What makes this a happy place? How do you feel that in your body? It can be an existing place in your current life, or it can be an imaginary place or something from the past.

2. Keep your eyes closed and let go of that happy place or let it fade away and now visualise an unpleasant situation that you experienced recently. Really put yourself back into that moment, as if you were really there right now. Who is there with you and what is happening now? What are you doing and what are the others doing? What do you see, hear or smell? What do you feel and think? What do you feel in your body? Go to the moment when you start feeling really bad.

3. Concentrate on that bad feeling and release the image of that situation or let it fade away. But hold on to that feeling and ask yourself if you recognise it. Then consider whether you ever felt this way in your childhood. You don't have to actively search for a very similar situation. A memory might also pop up unexpectedly. Just wait and see if a memory comes up, while you hold on to the feeling.

4. If a memory from your childhood comes to mind, try to visualise that situation as well as you can. You are probably still a child, so you are small and the others are big. What happens now? What do you see, hear or smell? What do you feel and think?

5. What would you like to see happen to change or stop this unpleasant situation? Is there anyone who can help you? Or is there nothing you can do about it? You are often unable to identify what is needed because you are just a child.

6. Go back to the happy place where you started the exercise for a moment.

7. Stop the exercise by opening your eyes.

8. Write down what you discovered. What is the connection between that unpleasant situation in the present and the situation in the past? What were you afraid of, or angry or sad about? What did you think as a child? For example, did you feel inferior, abandoned, threatened or restricted in your actions? Were demands made that were too high or did you feel guilty? It could be anything.

A therapist first explains the exercise and then guides it in the sequence above. She will ask you to tell her what you see in your imagination and help you put yourself into that situation as well as you can. During this exercise, you can always tell her what you are experiencing. The main goal is for you to imagine yourself in the situation as well as possible and experience what you feel and think. After the exercise, you and the therapist will discuss the connection between the situation then and now and what pitfalls and modes could have developed from that situation. If you do this exercise independently, try using the description of the pitfalls and modes to discover what connection might exist.

Example: Visualisation exercise to discover pitfalls and modes with Martin

Martin says he called in sick at work after being saddled with far too many tasks and not daring to refuse. He feels guilty that now his colleagues have to take over his work.

T: Martin, you talk about being given too many tasks and not daring to say no. Let's explore why by doing the visualisation exercise I told you about earlier. So we'll go back to that situation in your imagination to see if we can figure out why this is so difficult for you.

M: (agrees)

T: Just close your eyes, and try to imagine a happy place where you feel at ease and nothing is expected of you.

M: I'm sitting at home on the sofa with the cat on my lap.

T: Do you see the cat lying on your lap? Do you feel where he's lying? Are you stroking him? How do you feel?

M: Yes, I'm stroking him and he's purring ... I feel relaxed and cosy with the cat on my lap.

T: OK, now keep your eyes closed, and let go of that happy place, or let it fade away. Now visualise the moment when your supervisor wants to give you the extra tasks. Immerse yourself in the situation completely, as if you were really there. Do you see him? What does he say?

M: He says a lot of people are off sick, and that he expects me to step up.

T: Do you see where the supervisor is standing? Where are you standing or sitting? How does his voice sound?

M: I'm sitting, and he's standing in the doorway. He sounds rather hurried and abrupt.

T: How do you feel now? What are you thinking? What is happening?

M: I feel nervous, but I don't think I can refuse because it is true that many people are sick. So I say that I'll try.

T: Where do you feel that in your body?

M: Pressure on the chest.

T: Focus on that tense feeling, but let the image of this situation fade away. Hold on to that tense feeling and ask yourself whether you ever felt this way in your childhood … You don't have to actively look for a very similar situation to this. Maybe a memory will pop up unexpectedly. Just hold on to your feeling and wait calmly. See if a memory arises spontaneously.

M: I can see a situation now where my mother asks me to go shopping, but I also have a lot of homework.

T: Are you back in that situation? How old are you?

M: About eight.

T: Where is your mother and where are you? Take a look at your mother. What do you see?

M: I'm sitting at the kitchen table with my homework in front of me, and she walks into the kitchen. She looks tired.

T: Do you say anything to your mother about the homework?

M: Yes, cautiously … But my mother is having a hard enough time as it is, because my sister is ill. I see that she's tired and has a headache.

T: What would you like to see happen to change or stop this unpleasant situation? Is there anyone who can help you? Or is there nothing you can do about it?

M: I would like my sister to get better. But that's not possible. There's no one who can help my mother. If I don't do it, we won't have dinner later.

> T: OK. Now we'll finish the exercise. Just go back to the
>   happy place from before, when you were sitting on the
>   sofa with your cat on your lap … once you're back
>   there and feeling a little better, you can open your eyes.
>
> In the follow-up discussion, Martin discovers that he often
> gets sick when there are problems at work. He doesn't say no
> and tries to adapt as best he can (the subordinate), but he is
> very afraid of doing it wrong (the dependent, failing child).
> This is because mother always used to call on him or his
> brother to help her. His brother often refused, but not
> Martin. He always felt much too responsible, and his father
> also told him to help his mother: after all, she was struggling
> (guilt-inducing mode). The modes mentioned here will
> return later in Martin's mode model (Figure 3.1, p. 84).

5.   Getting to know modes using chairs

The therapist can also clarify which modes are at play in a
difficult situation by giving them each their own chair. She first
listens to what you relate about a problem you have experienced
and pays close attention to how you tell it. She indicates that she
thinks one of your modes is coming to the forefront now and
then suggests that you move that mode to another chair. For
example, if she thinks your vulnerable child is speaking, she may
ask you to sit in another chair and, from there, from your vulnerable child's perspective, tell her what you would like or need
(for example more rest).

If you then say that none of that is possible anyway because
you haven't finished your duties yet, she asks you to sit in another
chair and let that side of yourself (your demanding mode) say
why what you really want (more rest) is not on the cards right
now, because you have to finish your work first. On another

occasion, your avoidant coping mode may be most prominent and then the therapist may suggest that you sit in a different chair and talk about the problem from that avoidant coping mode.

Exercise 3.2

Getting to know modes using chairs

1. You talk about a problem you experienced in the past week.
2. The therapist hears the mode from which you tell the story. She says which mode she believes is now at the forefront.
3. The therapist asks if you want to sit in a different chair to say how you view the problem from that mode.
4. The therapist asks you (in this mode) a number of questions to clarify what this mode involves, and again names which mode it is.
5. The therapist asks you to sit back in the chair you were sitting on before.
6. You discuss whether you recognise that this is one part of yourself. The therapist explains which mode this is. Together, you give this mode a name.

The purpose of this exercise is to make you realise that you have different modes, and they all have their own influence on what you feel, think and do. Child modes are usually characterised by intense feelings because you perceive that your needs are not being met. The critical modes are constantly on you with negative criticism. The purpose of coping modes is to protect you from these negative influences and act as if the fact that your needs are not being met is no big deal.

In this way, you can also independently try to get a clearer picture of the different aspects of your personality.

Example of Sarah

Sarah has had a busy week at work and takes work home on Friday to finish over the weekend. She notices that she is very tired and would have to cancel fun activities on weekends. She decides to use two chairs to explore why she feels such pressure to work through the weekend. Chair 1 is in favour of the idea that she should continue working, chair 2 is against that idea. Sarah keeps switching chairs.

In Chair 1:   I have to complete these tasks for Monday, otherwise the work will keep piling up and there will be more new tasks on Monday.

In Chair 2:   But I've already been working way too hard for weeks, I also need to relax once in a while.

In Chair 1:   You promised your colleagues that it would be ready last week.

In Chair 2:   That's true, but I did that because that other colleague said she didn't have time. She did then take the weekend off. She also values her family and keeps weekends free, as a rule. Why don't I do that? Which mode is this?

Sarah takes time to reflect and realises that there is always a 'little voice in the back of her head' that says it is never good enough and that she always needs to step it up a notch. She thinks that 'little voice' is in chair 1 and that it is her demanding mode.

This way of working with chairs is a bit strange to most people at first. Why should you sit in a different chair when a certain mode of yours is at the forefront? Scientific research and the experience in schema therapy show that it is a useful way to gain more insight into the different sides of yourself, enabling you to try to change these modes later (Wijngaart, 2020). I describe working with chairs in more detail in Chapter 4.

Making your mode model

After four to six therapy sessions, when it has become clear which behavioural patterns keep leading to problems and which modes play a role in them, you create a model showing the connection between your different modes. That model should incorporate all your modes as well as the interactions between them.

A simple model (see Appendix 1) at least describes what your child mode and critical mode are and which coping modes make you feel the pain of the vulnerable child less and hear your critical voice less. In the same model, you also indicate how big or small an influence your healthy adult mode and your happy child mode have. Finally, come up with your own names for all your modes.

The simple model is appropriate if you only have one variant of a critical mode and your child mode consists of one of the vulnerable child modes and/or angry child modes. In that case, you probably only have one or two coping modes. Put the types of avoidance and inversion together in one circle.

A complex model (see Appendix 1) includes more critical, child and coping modes. A child mode may then consist of two or three parts (a vulnerable child, an angry child and an impulsive child). The critical mode can also have two or three parts (demanding, punitive and/or guilt-inducing). You can also have more than one coping mode: variants of an avoidant and/or inversion coping mode. Put those variants of each coping mode together in a circle.

The models the therapist creates together with Martin and Nora (Figures 3.3 on p. 86 and Figure 3.1 on p. 84), and the model created by Sarah herself (Figure 3.2 on p. 85), are only examples. Of course, the idea is that you work out a model that fits you well. You can use the 'Mode Model Worksheet' in Appendix 1 to do this.

For Nora, the healthy adult and the happy child are drawn smaller than the other modes because they are very weakly developed at the moment. Nora often does not know how to solve things in an adult way, which is why she keeps losing her jobs and struggles with relationships. As soon as she tries to do something right, the punitive mode (Nora calls it 'the Witch') immediately starts to lay into her, eventually making her angry or anxious or sad. This is symbolised by the arrow from 'the Witch' to angry Nora and little Nora. To escape these unpleasant feelings, she falls back on her coping modes: shutting down her feelings completely by putting up a wall (avoidant coping mode) or acting tough (inversion coping mode). She calls these coping modes 'the Wall' and 'the Tough Girl', respectively. That the coping modes serve to protect her is symbolically represented by a dotted line between the intense feelings of 'the Witch' and little Nora on the one hand and the coping modes on the other.

If you create a mode model for yourself, you may end up with more modes than are currently described for Nora. For example, you can have a demanding mode in addition to a punitive mode. Then put them both in the top circle (see Sarah's and Martin's mode models). As you see with Nora (in Figure 3.2), you can also have more than one coping mode. Then draw two circles to the left of the dotted line: one for the avoidant coping mode and one for the inversion coping mode. You usually place all the avoidant coping modes together in one circle. You do the same for the inversion coping modes. You also give those groups of modes their own names. For Nora, the avoidant coping modes are collectively called 'the Wall' and the inversion coping modes 'the Tough Girl'. You can also give these modes different names.

A plan to change your modes

Once you have identified the problems and have represented them in the mode model, you can make a plan to change your modes. Whether you're working on your problems with a therapist or independently, now it is time to concretely describe how you will approach this.

The specific change plan is different for each individual (a therapist usually calls it a treatment plan), but the overarching goal is the same for everyone: to strengthen the healthy adult and the happy child as much as possible. To achieve that, you will do the following:

1. Fulfil the needs of the vulnerable child
2. Teach the angry child to deal with anger
3. Limit the impulsive, undisciplined or spoilt child
4. Silence the critical modes
5. Make the avoidant and inversion coping modes less necessary
6. Develop the healthy adult
7. Give the happy child much more space.

You will work on all these sub-goals in Chapter 5.

You also need to determine how much time you think you'll need for this. A therapist indicates how long the treatment will take. Depending on the severity of the problems, this will be one to two years: changing modes takes time.

Timeframe

The therapist tells **Martin** that he would like to have an appointment with him every week for a year and then once a month for another year.

Nora's treatment begins intensively, with two appointments per week in the first year. The second year, she will start with one appointment per week, and the frequency will then be gradually reduced further.

For **Sarah**, it is advisable not to drive for superfast change, because that is precisely her problem: she wants too much and does everything at a fast pace. Her friend therefore helps her set realistic goals. Together, they come to the conclusion that she should allot at least a year for the change process.

Martin and Nora's therapists give them homework in between appointments to read Chapters 2 and 3 of this book and ask them to pay attention to situations in which they started to feel worse, and make a note of it.

Difficult moments

At some point, everyone doubts their approach and their progress in the change process. These doubts are usually linked to the reason you sought help. That is why we give a few more examples of doubts that Sarah, Martin and Nora had when they started the process of changing modes.

Difficult moments when you start discovering modes

Sarah is already a hard worker. Just when she tries to start working on her modes, she is offered a new job with even more challenges and even more work. It is tempting, but this is precisely her pitfall. She wanted to change her modes because she noticed that she already works way too much and has no time left over for her family and friends. Her friend points this out to her when discussing the step-by-step plan with her. It is hard for Sarah to accept, but then she decides to seriously explore why, despite her intentions, she is tempted to accept a new, even more demanding job.

Martin usually comes to the sessions faithfully, but after a few times he does cancel unexpectedly, giving the reason that he feels ill. However, the therapist suspects there is more to it. Based on what he already knows about Martin, he thinks something is bothering Martin that he is afraid to discuss with him. Perhaps the tensions this generates are the root cause of Martin's physical symptoms. He calls Martin and motivates him to come next time anyway and to discuss what is holding him back.

The following week, the truth comes out: Martin is used to asking everyone for advice and support and finds it very difficult that the therapist does not react like almost everyone around him. He is used to others advising him or taking things over for him when he says he doesn't know or can't do something. He's annoyed that the therapist doesn't do this, but didn't initially dare to call him on it – after all, he has learnt to adapt to other people.

The therapist understands Martin's need for advice because he knows Martin is used to that. He discusses with him whether things might be moving a bit too fast and whether the therapy is more difficult than Martin had expected. He then explains that one of the treatment goals is precisely for Martin to become more independent and learn to choose what he wants for himself. He indicates that this will not work if, as the therapist, he takes over the role of advisor from his family and friends. That would only perpetuate his mode. However, the therapist does promise to try to only gradually change that mode with him.

Nora finds herself in a crisis after the first few appointments because she has a massive quarrel with Frank. She thinks he'll leave her and has the tendency to drink to suppress her anxiety. The therapist uses this situation to investigate which modes are involved:

- Little Nora is afraid that she couldn't handle it if Frank breaks up with her.
- 'The Witch' says these problems are all her own fault.
- So 'the Wall' comes to protect her by drinking.

The therapist creates a crisis plan with Nora to describe what Nora can do when her child modes 'the Witch' and 'the Wall' or 'the Tough Girl' threaten to take the reins. It includes what she can do to calm down and who she can ask for help. It also says that she can call the therapist if she gets so upset between appointments that there is a threat she will do things that are dangerous to her (such as harming herself or using too much alcohol or drugs) or to others (such as hurting her boyfriend).

If you are tempted to drop out, of course a therapist will try to explore with you what is bothering you and do her best to motivate you to continue therapy. Difficult moments can almost always be resolved when you discuss what is bothering you with your therapist or a friend. Indeed, talking about it can strengthen your bond with them and probably help you understand your modes better.

***

Step 1 Overview briefly summarises all the elements of discovering your own modes again. First, it describes the role of the therapist and what you can do as a client. It then describes what you can do independently with the help of a friend.

Chapter 4 covers the second step, in which you learn to recognise your modes in everyday situations.

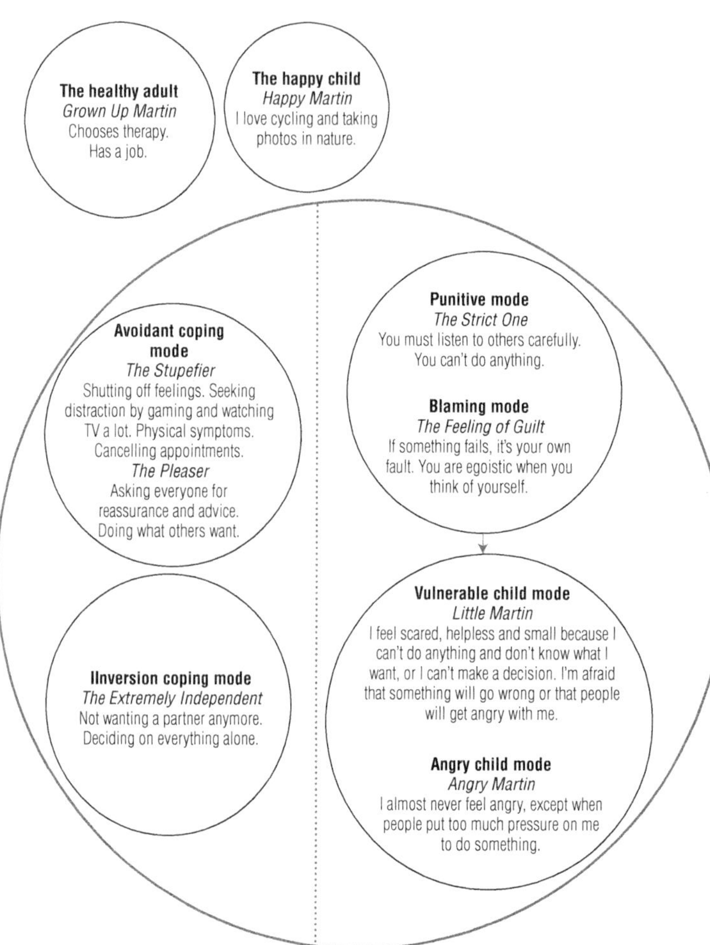

Figure 3.1   Martin's mode model

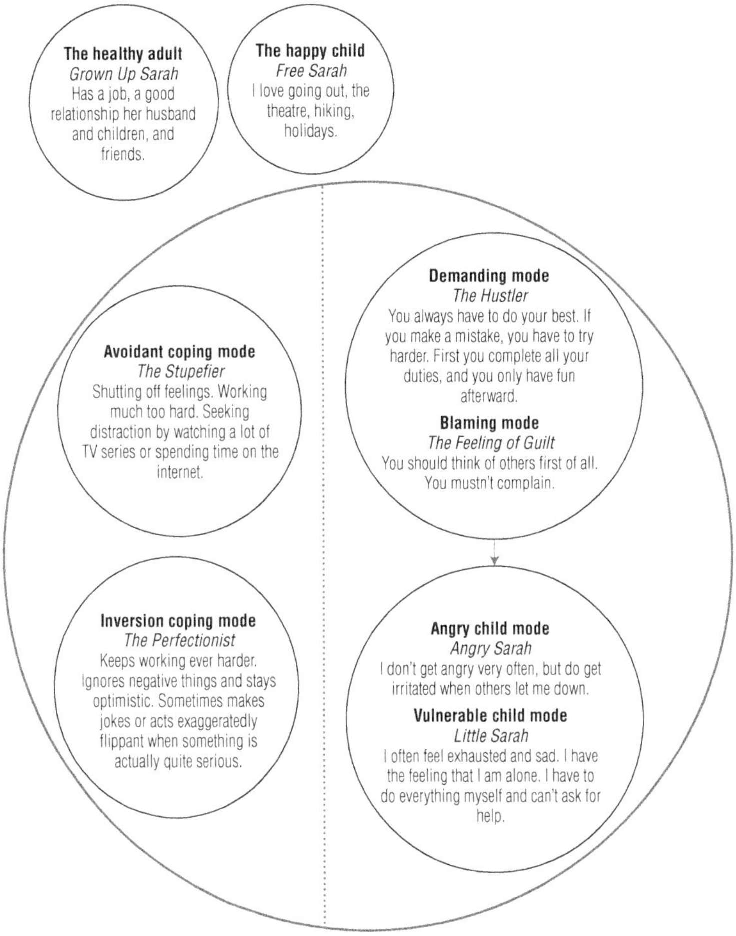

Figure 3.2   Sarah's mode model

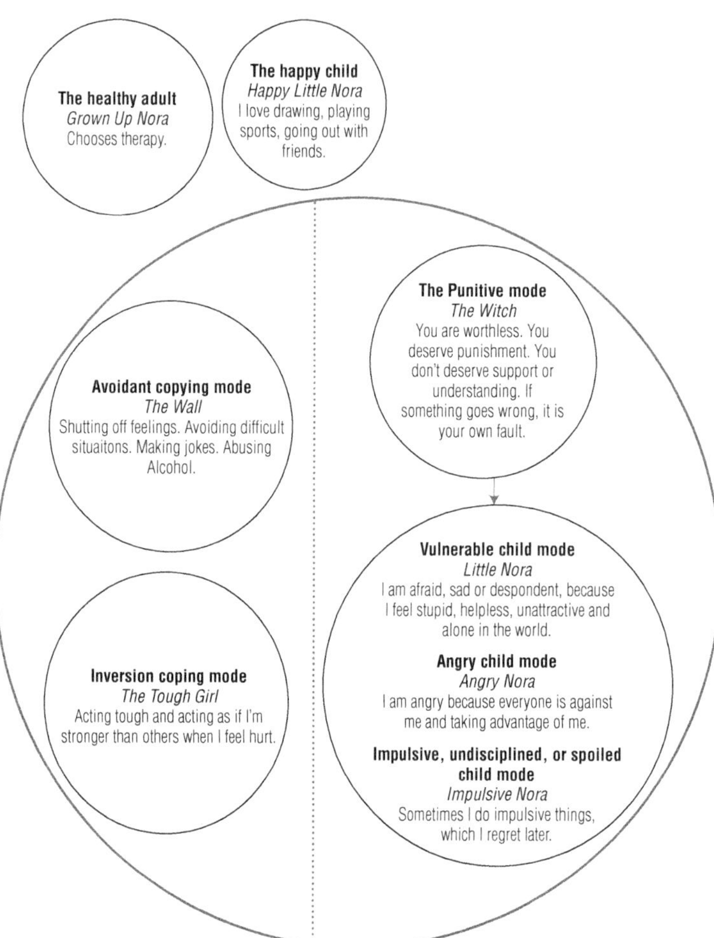

Figure 3.3   Nora's mode model

Step 1 Overview

Discovering your own modes (usually takes four to seven weeks)

Section	Therapist	Client	You do it yourself	Friend
Inventory of problems	Asks what problems you are running into.	Tells what the problems are.	You write down what your problems are.	Talks to you about your problems.
Translation of problems into modes	Takes an example and identifies different modes that play a role in it.	Gives information and asks questions.	You take an example and identify different modes of yourself in it.	Discusses the examples with you and adds to them if necessary.
Linking modes to your life history	Gathers relevant information from the past about the influence of caregivers and others.	Provides information on family and relevant events in childhood.	You describe your life history. You ask questions to family members and old friends.	Thinks about your life history with you.
Filling in questionnaires	Provides a questionnaire about pitfalls and a questionnaire about modes.	Fills in questionnaires.	You fill in the questionnaires.	Discusses the results with you. Also fills in the questionnaires themselves.
Visualisation exercise	Does a visualisation exercise to discover connections between current problems and the past.	Participates in the exercise and discovers connections to the past.	You do a visualisation exercise and discover connections to the past.	
Using chairs to get to know modes	Does the exercise with chairs.	Participates in the exercise with chairs.	You do the exercise with chairs.	

Discovering your own modes (usually takes four to seven weeks)

Section	Therapist	Client	You do it yourself	Friend
Creating an overview of all the modes	Creates a mode model together with the client.	Participates in the mode model and indicates how he/she sees it.	You make a mode model.	Discusses the model with you and adds to it if necessary.
Plan to change your modes	Explains that the treatment is about the present and past and the steps needed to change the modes. Indicates how long the treatment will take.	Agrees or disagrees with this treatment plan and makes time for treatment. Reads Chapter 1 of this book.	You make a plan for the change process and make time for it. You read Chapter 1 of this book.	Discusses the plan with you. Encourages you to keep going. Reads Chapter 1 of this book to better understand what you are working on.
Homework	Gives homework to read Chapters 2 and 3.	Reads Chapters 2 and 3 of this book.	You read Chapters 2 and 3.	Reads Chapters 2 and 3.
Difficult moments	Crisis or acute social problems, or requests for practical help, can disrupt the inventory.	Indicates what he/she finds difficult at this stage or exhibits behaviour that hinders the progress of therapy.	Something happens that triggers your pitfalls.	Can warn you to watch out that the problem doesn't get bigger, leaving you without any more time to change your modes.
Tips for difficult moments	Doesn't succumb to the temptation to start solving acute problems, keeps analysing the modes in this type of problem. Discusses difficult moments with colleagues.	Tries to continue therapy. Crisis is influenced by his/her modes. Tries to trust that the therapist is going to help him/her.	You consider what is best for you if you want to change modes in the coming year.	Thinks about the modes at play here. Can remind you of similar behaviour in the past.

4

Step 2: Recognising modes
in everyday situations

In Chapter 3, you learnt to translate your problems into modes, gave names to those different modes of yourself and worked out a mode model for yourself. Now it's time for the next step: you will discover when you react from one of the unhelpful modes and when your reaction is the product of the healthy adult or the happy child.

If you don't have any major problems but do have some disruptive behaviour patterns, you usually react as your healthy adult or happy child. This is the case with Sarah, for example who wants to change her modes herself. But if you regularly experience problems in your relationships with other people and frequently feel uncomfortable, or even very bad, then the other three unhelpful modes are often prevalent. However, everyone will find that unhelpful modes are active more often than they previously realised.

It's not easy to become aware of the fact that you have fallen short in some areas and feel unhappy as a result. Especially when old memories are brought up that you tried to forget. Even so, it is also often a relief to start understanding why you don't handle some things deftly and why others sometimes react negatively to you. On the other hand, however, this is not suddenly going to make you feel better: unfortunately, it's not that easy to change modes. Realise that this is only the second step in your change process and keep in mind that change is indeed coming.

This second step will usually take you three to six weeks. After that, you will actually start addressing your modes. But first we keep the focus on recognising your modes in everyday situations. We illustrate how to do this with the examples of Sarah, Martin and Nora.

Learning to recognise modes

Sarah will keep track of the situations in which she tends to overwork, watch TV series or browse the internet to release her stress. She is trying to understand what is actually going on in those moments. To do this, she always keeps her mode model handy to have an indication of the modes that could be activated. In this way, she discovers that this tendency is greater when she regards something as having gone wrong at work or in her family. She doesn't understand very well yet why she gets grumpy and works even harder in such situations.

Her friend notes that it could well be 'the Hustler' (demanding mode), fussing over every detail and telling her to try harder. Little Sarah then feels ashamed of herself and resolves to try harder the next day ('the Perfectionist') and seeks distraction ('the Stupefier') instead of discussing her problems with others.

Martin has trouble recognising modes because he actually likes the fact that other people help him so much and he also likes helping other people. But he does suffer a lot from his physical symptoms and doesn't quite understand where they come from. He keeps track of when his symptoms increase and decrease and what preceded that.

Together with Martin, the therapist examines what came before a moment when the symptoms increased, which did cause certain modes to be activated without Martin realising it. They also use Martin's mode model as aid for this. In this way, they discover that they occur more often when 'the Pleaser' makes a great effort to make others happy (avoidant coping mode). Then, when the other person still isn't satisfied, the feeling of guilt (guilt-inducing mode) becomes active and he starts feeling bad again anyway (Little Martin: the dependent, failing Martin). This causes him tension, which can manifest itself as increased physical symptoms. The therapist explains that while these modes seem to work in the short term (people are usually happy that he is so helpful and friendly), in the longer term they cause exhaustion and physical stress symptoms.

It often happens that **Nora** gets very angry or upset when someone cancels an appointment or when Frank wants to do something with his friends without her. She immediately thinks they don't like her and will abandon her. This makes sense in her view because she is actually a stupid person. Then she pretends it doesn't matter to her and says she doesn't want anything to do with them anymore.

Together with her therapist, she looks for modes in these situations using her mode model. The therapist explains that for Nora, the basic needs of acceptance, connection, security and predictability were not met, which immediately makes her think the other person doesn't think she is worthwhile. This makes her sad (little Nora) and angry (angry Nora). Then 'the Witch' (her punitive mode) makes things worse by suggesting that she is now being punished for being a nasty person. To avoid feeling the pain this causes, her tough mode quickly activates, and she pretends that none of this matters to her. She usually closes herself off from others and the world for quite a long time afterwards to avoid repeating the pain ('the Wall').

For Nora, several modes are activated in quick succession. This makes it even more difficult for her to recognise them and tell them apart. In these cases, the therapist encourages her to write down what happened, and try to translate it into her various modes herself. During the session, the therapist also works with her to explore where the activated modes came from; in other words, which experiences in her childhood led to these modes.

The examples show that it helps to use your mode model as an aid and have someone else help think about your modes in problematic situations. You can also use the 'Mode Model Worksheet' in Appendix 1 to write down what your different modes look like and the typical situations that lead to their activation.

(See Chapter 2 for a detailed description of each mode. You can also download the corresponding mode worksheets for free at https://www.wiley.com/go/breakingnegativepatterns/1e.

In the beginning, you might still find it difficult to distinguish between the different modes because this is a new way for you to look at your problems. But with the help of your therapist or a friend, you will get better at this. You'll learn to recognise why you sometimes get into trouble and hopefully gain some compassion for yourself against the backdrop of the circumstances that shaped you.

Aids in recognising your modes

In addition to the mode model, the therapist, or you yourself, can do the exercise with the chairs (Exercise 3.2, p. 75) or use the visualisation exercise (Exercise 3.1, p. 70) to translate a problematic situation into modes.

For example, if your coping mode is very strong, it might make sense to put it in a different chair and interview it as a way to emphasise that one of your modes is active and to explore why it is now rearing its head. You act as if that mode is a person who wants to protect you, and you ask him why he does that. What is he protecting you from? Are you afraid you'll be overwhelmed by negative feelings? Are you afraid the critical mode might gain the upper hand? Do you not trust your therapist? The more often you subject your modes to this kind of examination, the more easily you will learn to recognise them.

If your child mode is causing intense emotions, it may be useful to do a visualisation exercise where you transition from the situation that is affecting you so much now to a situation in your childhood. This enables you to make connections between the present and your past. With this method, you might also find out, for example that you are still dependent on your parents because they never taught you to become independent.

Visualisation exercise with Martin

The first times the therapist does a visualisation exercise with Martin (see p. 71), they are not yet able to bring the basic needs that weren't sufficiently met in his childhood into focus. The therapist notes that Martin was given very many responsibilities at a very young age. Martin responds by defending his parents. After all, they couldn't help the fact that his sister was often ill and his mother needed his help. Over time, however, he discovers that his parents' good intentions sometimes overshot into patronising, which is why he still often thinks he can't do anything today.

When taking stock of the modes, the therapist used a chair exercise to demonstrate that you have several modes that are not helping you solve your problems in your current life (Exercise 3.2, p. 75). If you want to discover your modes in everyday situations, take the mode model and use the names you have given to the different modes. As an example, see the mode models for Nora, Martin and Sarah at the end of Chapter 3. Let's see how this worked for Martin.

Discovering modes using chairs with Martin

Martin's mother has asked him to help clean up the basement. Martin doesn't actually want to do that. He already helps her a lot with chores and errands, but it is never enough. Actually, he is tired and wants to do something relaxing. But he's afraid to tell his mother this because he would feel guilty. The therapist suggests that they explore Martin's mode responsible for that feeling: his guilt-inducing mode, which they have dubbed 'the Feeling of Guilt'. He grabs an extra chair and asks Martin to sit in that chair and play 'the Feeling of Guilt'.

T: Now that you're sitting in that chair, you can try to say how 'the Feeling of Guilt' feels about the fact that Martin could say no to his mother.

M: You can't do that, after all, your mother has always been there for you. So now you have to help her too.

T: So Martin should go and help his mother anyway, even if he is tired?

M: Yes, it's not that much trouble, is it? Do good, have good.

T: Martin, will you stand up now and leave 'the Feeling of Guilt' on that chair? Come and sit next to me again.

T: How do you feel in this chair when you hear that mode of yours (points to the empty chair where 'the Feeling of Guilt' sits) saying that you do have to help?

> M: Tired and disheartened. It is never enough.
>
> T: So you have one mode that thinks you have to do it because you'd be a bad son if you didn't (points to the chair where 'the Feeling of Guilt' sits) and then you have a mode that feels you are tired and don't want to do it. That's little Martin, who feels that it's too much, but is afraid to say so because the feeling of guilt is too strong. And I think there's also a mode that always adapts to others to avoid problems. We call that 'the Pleaser'. (The therapist adds an extra chair.) Go sit there. What does this mode say?
>
> M: (sits down in the other chair) That I'd better get over my fatigue, because then I won't disappoint my mother. That way, I'll also prevent her from sighing and complaining, which makes me feel bad.
>
> T: 'The Pleaser' seems to solve the problem in the short term, by helping anyway. That way, you try to avoid 'the Feeling of Guilt' becoming active. But in the long run, 'the Pleaser' makes it that little Martin's need for rest and having fun is not fulfilled.

With the different modes placed on separate chairs, Martin starts to recognise these modes and realises how these modes affect his actions. He cannot change them yet, but that will come in Step 3.

Homework

The homework during this period is that you regularly, preferably every day, use your mode model to try to describe and analyse a situation in which you had difficulties. Describe what happened and what you felt, thought and did and translate that into your different modes. Don't worry if you don't always manage it yet: in effect, you're learning a new language, and that takes practice. If you're in therapy, at least take a description of one or more situations to the next session. The therapist will then help you make the translation.

Difficult moments

In this phase, the difficult moments are usually primarily related to becoming aware of the severity of your problems, which might exacerbate the unpleasant feelings because you start feeling more. In response, your coping modes could actually gain in strength to ward off those unpleasant feelings. You may also find it difficult to have patience for the change process and feel that things are not moving fast enough for you.

Difficult moments when trying to recognise modes in everyday situations

Sarah is becoming increasingly aware of her tendency to do too much and relax too little, but does not know how to change that. Her demanding mode feels that the desired change is not progressing fast enough. As a result, she feels increasingly worked up and tends to try even harder. When she discusses this with her friend, the friend shows compassion for her feelings and tries to reassure her. She says that change comes step by step, and that pushing harder and harder is an old coping mode ('the Perfectionist') that doesn't help in the long run.

Martin experiences more physical symptoms because the therapist does not help him with advice. He is inclined to cancel appointments. Now that he keeps a diary of when his physical symptoms increase or decrease, he does increasingly clearly recognises a pattern and realises that cancelling appointments with his therapist actually stems from his old coping mode ('the Stupefier'). Holding on to that will not help him, he realises. The therapist does understand Martin's avoidant coping mode and explains that this strategy did help him effectively in the past, which is why it is so persistent. Moreover, Martin doesn't know how to do things differently yet, given that the therapy has only just begun. The therapist encourages him to continue therapy.

Nora finds that her problems are not improving fast enough. She is still having one relationship crisis after another. Apparently the therapist can't solve that either. On the one hand she feels increasingly sad and angry; on the other hand sometimes she suddenly doesn't feel

> anything at all. Or, on the contrary, she acts very tough and denies needing help.
>
> The therapist encourages her to contact her in crisis situations so she can support her when she is upset. At this stage, an extra session or telephone contact is occasionally needed to calm Nora down. When Nora comes across as 'numb' in her contact with the therapist, she tries to make it clear to her that this is the coping mode 'the Wall' or 'the Tough Girl'. She explains that these coping modes arose in the past because it was actually dangerous for Nora to show her feelings then. She emphasises that one of the goals of therapy is for these modes to become less active over time as Nora comes to understand that she is safe with the therapist. She encourages her to continue therapy.

This phase of recognising modes without attempting to address them does not usually last longer than six weeks. Quite quickly, you take action to change the modes. Nevertheless, during the next steps, you will still continue to investigate which modes are activated within you because you are still far from realising it every time. Even long after therapy has concluded, it is worthwhile to stay alert to activation of modes in difficult situations. Indeed, under extreme circumstances, old modes may return unexpectedly. Fortunately, you will have caught on much earlier and know what to do to mobilise the healthy adult to support and comfort your vulnerable child.

***

Step 2: Overview recapitulates all the steps you take to recognise your own modes in everyday situations.

The following chapters deal with the last three steps: breaking through your modes and how to sustain those changes.

Step 2 Overview

Recognising modes in everyday situations (usually takes three to six weeks)

Section	Therapist	Client	You do it yourself	Friend
Discussing problem	Helps in recognising modes.	Sometimes unexpected things happen. Sometimes nothing seems wrong. Sometimes it is difficult for the client.	You write down a difficult situation every day. You try to recognise modes.	If you can't find a mode, she helps think about it.
Exercise	Does an exercise to clarify connections between past and present.	Does not recognise modes, especially when he or she is in a coping mode. Does not see links with the past.	You occasionally try an exercise.	Listens to your experiences.
Homework	Asks the client to regularly, preferably every day, use his mode model to describe and analyse a situation in which he had difficulties.	Describes difficult situations and translates them into modes.	You describe difficult situations and translate them into modes.	Helps you with the translation to modes.

Difficult moments	Notices that the client's tendency not to feel is very strong under the influence of coping modes.	Has difficulty with the therapist's insistence on pushing the coping mode aside so that he or she will feel more.	You become more aware of your modes, but find that you start feeling worse rather than better.	
Tips for difficult moments	Tries to continue with schema therapy. Realises that the client once badly needed his coping mode, but does not yet realise that it is no longer a help to him now.	For example, tries to understand the role of different modes in past and present life, especially when he or she acts too tough or shuts off his or her feelings.	You discuss problems and feelings with your friend.	Listens to you and shows understanding. Doesn't judge too quickly and focuses on asking about feelings.

5

Step 3: Starting to change modes

Now that you have discovered your modes (Step 1) and can recognise them in everyday situations (Step 2), the emphasis is now explicitly on change. Step 3 takes 18–28 weeks, depending on the persistence of your modes. It is best to read through this chapter in full before you start practising.

In Chapter 3, we mentioned that the goal of treatment is the same for everyone: to strengthen your healthy adult and your happy child as much as possible. We also explained that this overarching goal can be divided into seven sub-goals:

1. Fulfil the needs of the vulnerable child
2. Teach the angry child to deal with anger
3. Limit the impulsive, undisciplined or spoilt child
4. Silence the critical modes
5. Make the avoidant and inversion coping modes less necessary
6. Develop the healthy adult
7. Give the happy child much more space

These seven sub-goals, combined with your mode model, form the basis of the treatment plan. If you are working with a therapist, you will draw up this plan together. The therapist will work with you to help make the sub-goals concrete, and discuss the steps for you to work on them. If, like Sarah, you are working on changing modes by yourself, you have to create the treatment plan yourself. This is a matter of figuring out how to work on the seven goals for yourself. Wherever this chapter refers to 'the therapist', you should read this as 'me' or 'my healthy adult'.

There are many people like Sarah who have a strong healthy adult. Especially with support from one or more friends who help to discover their blind spots, they are able to achieve their goals independently. However, if you lacked too much in your childhood, like Nora and Martin, it might be wise to find a schema therapist on www.schematherapysociety.com or a schema therapy site of your country like www.schematherapie.nl or schematherapievlaanderen.be.

A closer look at the seven sub-goals

The treatment plan aims to finally fulfil the unmet basic emotional needs and make the healthy adult and happy child stronger. This is done by working on the modes named in your mode model. We describe how the desired change takes shape for each of the seven sub-goals below.

1.   Fulfilling the needs of the vulnerable child

As you know by now, you are in one of the child modes when you submit to your pitfalls (see Tables 2.2–2.4). These pitfalls are linked to basic needs that were inadequately met in your childhood. Because of this, you try to connect with the vulnerable child within yourself and start learning how to take care of that child as a good parent. For many people, this isn't as easy as it sounds. They have few memories of their childhood or think they were a difficult child and so it was their own fault that they were treated badly. Some people even resent the vulnerable child in themselves and reject their own feelings. It is important that you discover what you were like as a child, and what you experienced, in order to gain a better understanding of the child you were and to find out what you needed back then.

If you don't know how to care for your vulnerable child yourself yet, during the therapy exercises the therapist will take on the role of a 'good parent' who does fulfil your basic needs. So if you think you're stupid because you've done something wrong, she doesn't react angrily but shows compassion for the situation and helps you think of how to handle it better next time. A good parent is not a perfect parent, but more a kind of role model. That means that the therapist treats you as a normal parent would when their child has a problem. Such a parent provides support, comfort and explanation, and encourages you to be open about what you think, feel and think, and occasionally to try something out for yourself. They also teach you how to perform without setting the bar too high, sets limits when necessary and show you what is fair.

Caring for the vulnerable child is one of the main treatment goals because this helps you discover a healthy way to interact with yourself, others and the world. This gives you the space to develop your healthy adult and happy child.

2.   Teaching the angry child to deal with anger
The angry child's anger is usually a (too violent) reaction to what has been done to you or taken from you. When the angry child is at the forefront, the therapist always takes your anger seriously, even if you sometimes express it too violently. She teaches you that anger is a normal feeling and will help you express it earlier or differently than you are used to. This is relevant to Nora, for example. Her anger is like a volcanic eruption. If it's like that for you, the therapist can teach you to detect when your anger begins to rise so you can recognise it early on. You can then express your anger earlier as well, before it becomes a volcanic eruption.

On the other hand, it is also possible that you actually bottle up your anger too much and are afraid to express it. This sometimes results in physical ailments, as in Martin's case. In that case, the therapist will actually teach you to express your anger. First she helps you discover when you feel anger and what causes it. Then you learn how you can express anger in such a way that the other person actually notices that you are angry.

3.   Limiting the impulsive, undisciplined or spoilt child
If you have one of these child modes, then you did not learn to meet your basic needs in a balanced way. You fail to control your

impulses or to consider those around you when fulfilling your wishes and desires. Maybe you haven't learnt to deal with frustration and find it hard to swallow that you also have to do boring or tedious tasks like everyone else or can't handle it when something doesn't work right away. This leads to conflict and social rejection.

The key is to accept that fulfilling your needs is bound by limits and that you don't have more rights than other people. You need to learn to start and complete difficult tasks on time. This causes frustration in the short term, but in the long term, being considerate of those around you leads to social regard and much less conflict.

4.   Silencing the critical modes

This is about silencing your critical mode for good. As soon as you start talking negatively about yourself, the therapist will interrupt you and mention that she hears your punitive/demanding/guilt-inducing mode now. These critical modes don't actually help you and are the result of negative messages from people in your childhood. Their messages were not true then and aren't true now, but as a child you came to believe them anyway. Some people literally experience this as a voice in their head and for others they are mostly negative thoughts. Such a mode should already have been given its own name when the mode model was created, for example 'the Witch' or 'the Strict One'.

You have to learn to make a distinction between the critical mode and the healthy adult. Sometimes the healthy adult also thinks you handled something poorly, but has a nuanced way of thinking about it. He helps remind you of healthy rules for life and says things like: 'It's good to perform, but not to the point of burnout', 'Everyone makes mistakes; try to learn from them and do better in the future' or 'Considering others is different from adapting or subordinating yourself to them completely'. The critical mode and the healthy adult also strike a different tone: the former sounds harsh, negative and prescriptive, and the latter calm, reasonable and nuanced.

The treatment aims to silence the critical modes permanently because they are simplistic and exclusively negative.

5.   Making the avoidant and inversion coping modes less necessary

If a coping mode is active at the beginning of a session, the therapist will notice this quite quickly: they don't make contact with you, feel side-lined or are treated aggressively. All coping modes originated in your childhood as emergency solutions in difficult situations. As I described in detail in Chapter 2, there can be many forms of avoidant or inversion coping modes. The similarity between all these coping modes is that they are aimed at not feeling what you are lacking, in other words the basic needs that have remained unfulfilled. This often leads you to keep your distance from situations and people that are potentially dangerous to you. Unfortunately, this also keeps you away from the people who are well disposed towards you because you haven't learnt a balanced way to assess this. With this, you usually keep much too much distance from your therapist or friend as well. Coping modes are actually protective measures to prevent any setback or vulnerability that has gone too far.

The objective of the treatment is that these coping modes are needed less and less often. In other words, this means the healthy adult determines when it is wise to protect yourself, and the coping mode is not automatically activated every time. The therapist makes this possible on the one hand by supporting your vulnerable child, making it easier for you to lower your guard, and on the other hand by silencing your critical modes. With this the therapist prevents them from hurting your vulnerable child or triggering your angry child.

Like your critical mode, your coping mode has been given a name. So when your coping mode is active, you and your therapist refer to 'the Stupefier' or 'the Wall', for example. The therapist can then initiate the conversation with that mode to convince it to step aside so she can make contact with little Martin or little Nora. If this succeeds, the therapist can focus on fulfilling the vulnerable child's needs.

6.   Developing the healthy adult

Developing a healthy adult is a gradual process that continues throughout therapy. In the beginning, the healthy adult isn't that strong yet. That is why the therapist is a role model for this during each exercise. Starting from the next chapter (Step 4, Chapter 6), your own healthy adult is increasingly called upon during the exercises to support, comfort and help your own vulnerable child. The therapist then takes on a more coaching role. In the final step (Step 5, Chapter 7), the healthy adult is reinforced further as you experiment with it within and outside the therapy yourself. The therapist still encourages you, but leaves more and more to your healthy adult.

7.   Giving the happy child much more space

Creating space for the happy child is also done gradually. The more the healthy adult grows, the more room there will be for play and fun. However, that room for fun does not come about by itself, so the therapist challenges you to have fun alongside all your serious tasks both in the appointments and outside them.

How Sarah starts changing modes

Every other day, Sarah writes down when she thinks a mode was activated. Once a week, or more often if she finds it necessary, she sets aside an hour to work on one of these examples using chairs or a visualisation exercise. She regularly discusses with her friend what she has discovered and what she is struggling with.

How does an appointment with your therapist go?

What you discuss in therapy largely depends on your input. You should prepare for a therapy session by identifying what bothered you most in the past week. If you don't know that right away don't worry. Your therapist knows there are always issues that played out in earlier stages of your life and may suggest talking about them.

After you have described a problem in broad terms, your therapist will ask further questions and inquire about how you feel, but not immediately move on to practical solutions. The therapist will name the mode he suspects you are in at that moment and ask if you recognise it. For example, if you talk very flatly and unemotionally about a serious problem, you may be in an avoidant coping mode. On the other hand, if you are very emotional, your child mode is probably at the forefront. And if you talk particularly negatively about yourself, chances are that a critical mode has taken over. In short, the therapist can often hear which mode is active just by the way you say something.

Once it is clear which mode is predominant, the therapist suggests an exercise. This is often an experiential exercise, but sometimes a therapist will also go deeper into your thoughts. These exercises are new to you, so your therapist will explain the exercise clearly before you start. Once you get used to the exercises, you can skip the explanations and get straight to it. After the exercise, there should be time left over to discuss what you thought of it and what you got out of it.

TIP

It is a good idea to make an audio recording of each session and listen to it again at home. So much always happens in a conversation that it is difficult to remember or fully understand everything. Maybe you were in an avoidant coping mode for much of the conversation with your therapist so you didn't hear half of it! It is also useful to hear how your therapist addresses the different modes again. If you listen again at home, for example when your child mode or your healthy adult is active, you might hear more or something might suddenly strike you differently.

The following is an example of how the beginning of a session can go, using the experiences of Nora and Martin.

Start of a session with Nora

T: Good morning Nora, how is it going with you?

N: Good.

T: Did anything happen this week that you didn't feel that good about?

N: (flat tone) Yes, I did have problems again with the one woman I clean for, but anyway it's always the same. Maybe I should just quit that job.

T: I hear something is actually going on. You say that you experienced something unpleasant, but I notice that you tell it without much emotion. I think that means 'the Wall' is very active. Does that sound right?

N: Could be, but I really don't see the point in talking about this. (Nora is in her coping mode 'the Wall' so strongly that she identifies with it completely.)

T: Let's go through an exercise to explore why your coping mode, your 'Wall', is so strong. I suggest that we use chairs to do that.

T: Explains the exercise.

The beginning of a session with Martin

T: Good morning, Martin. How is it going with you?

M: Not that great. I haven't been able to prevent too much work being pushed onto me again. I worked through the whole weekend, and it still isn't finished.

T: It sounds quite critical, what you say about yourself.

M: Yes, but it makes sense though, I actually have been stupid enough not to set boundaries.

T: I don't think that does make much sense, but I do hear that your strict mode is speaking now. That's the mode that always says you're stupid and can't do anything. Does that sound right?

M: No, not really, because this time it really is stupid. (Martin is in his critical mode 'the Strict One' so strongly that he identifies with it completely.)

> T:　　I feel very sorry that strict Martin is being so nega-
> tive towards little Martin. I suggest that we do a
> visualisation exercise to explore where this criticism
> of yourself comes from. We'll go back in your
> imagination to the moment when you started
> thinking so negatively about yourself last week. But
> first, I'll explain to you exactly how the exercise goes.
>
> T:　　Explains the exercise.

Exercises to change your modes

You can change your modes in many different ways. For
maximum effect, it is important that you actually try different
ways. As I described in Chapter 2, there are exercises aimed at
your feelings (gaining new experiences), your thoughts (changing thoughts) and your behaviour (changing behaviour). In the
beginning, the emphasis is on thoughts and feelings. After that,
you focus much more on behaviour change, but you also continue to do experiential exercises and work on changing thoughts.

Gaining new experiences

Experiential exercises allow you to feel what it is like when your
needs do get met. If they have not been processed, nasty experiences from your childhood still affect how you feel today. You
can try to push those memories away using your coping modes,
but that doesn't work in the long run. Talking about it helps a
little bit. What works best are experiential exercises. There are
three types of experiential exercises: the visualisation exercise
(imagery), role-playing and working with chairs. Through these
exercises, you experience what it is like when someone does
come to help you in different ways, like a good parent would. In
this way, you get the support, comfort, explanation and encouragement that you lacked so badly as a child. You will also learn
how to tackle problems and what realistic boundaries are.

The visualisation exercise (imagery)

In a visualisation exercise, you imagine a (difficult) situation in the past, present or future. Brain research has shown that you react in almost the same way to something you experience in your imagination as to something that happens in reality, even if you know it that it didn't actually turn out that way.

During this third step of changing modes, you primarily go back to a period in your childhood when one or more of your basic needs were not met. That deficit may have arisen because your parents, teachers or others were unable to meet those needs or because of other negative experiences, such as bullying. This is how you discover that your persistent modes are the result of unpleasant situations in your childhood. In the beginning of the visualisation exercise, try to imagine what you were like as a child and what you experienced that made you feel so bad. But the moment you start feeling very bad, the therapist will step in to help and protect you.

Exercise 5.1

Visualisation of a pleasant situation

You usually start a visualisation exercise by imagining a pleasant situation, a place where you feel completely safe and at ease. This is also called the safe place and it is different for everyone. It can be a place in your current life (for example with the cat on your lap on the sofa) or a fantasy place (for example relaxing in the sun on a tropical beach). Try to imagine that situation as vividly as possible. When you do this, it helps if you sit comfortably and close your eyes. Also notice the smells and colours and what you feel in your body. Perhaps you feel the sun on your skin, or you smell the sea, or flowers. By immersing yourself well, you can really experience that sense of security and contentment, and your body will relax.

Exercise 5.2

Visualisation of a situation in your childhood

In your imagination, you can also go back to your childhood to discover what you were like as a child. If you are doing this for the first time, it is best to imagine a neutral or pleasant situation.

To do this exercise, find a quiet place where you can sit comfortably and easily with your feet on the ground. Make sure you are not disturbed for at least 20 minutes. First read through these instructions carefully. (Don't worry, you don't have to memorise the exercise or follow the steps exactly.) Then close your eyes and relax as well as you can.

Imagine going back to the house where you lived when you were about five or six years old. What is a nice place in that house? Is it your own room or another area? Are other people at home? Imagine an event you have pleasant memories of, for example your birthday or Christmas.

Freeze this image and enter the house as Grown-Up Me. Find Little Me and see what she looks like and how she is doing. Where is she? What does she look like? What is she doing? What do you want to say to her? How does she react to this encounter? Can you go do something fun together?

When you feel that all is well, take leave of Little Me again. Do you want to say anything else or give her something for the future? If so, do that.

Then slowly come back into the here and now. Check how your body feels. You are sitting in the chair with your feet on the floor and slowly open your eyes.

If it isn't that easy to imagine a pleasant situation in the house you lived in at the time, as is the case for Nora, it is better to use a photo of yourself as a child that you feel good about. You will usually prepare this together with your therapist. The therapist then asks you to bring a few photos of yourself as a small child and you choose one that you have fond memories of together.

Nora: visualisation of a situation in her childhood

T: Close your eyes and look at the photo of little Nora. Take a good look at what she looks like and look at her face. How does she feel in this situation?

N: I can see she's happy because she's playing with the dog at her grandma's house.

T: Now bring the picture to life and go to her. Is there anything you want to say to her?

N: Yes, I say: 'You're playing with the dog so nicely! What's his name?

T: How does she react? Is there anything you want to do with her that she likes?

N: She likes it that I'm there, and says his name is Bassie. I play with her and the dog. We take turns throwing the ball, and the dog runs after it.

T: When you feel that all is well, take leave of Little Nora. Do you want to say anything else or give her something for the future?

N: 'I really like playing with you and the dog. I'll come and see you more often'.

T: Okay, now slowly come back into the here and now. Check how your body feels. You are sitting in the chair with your feet on the floor and slowly open your eyes.

After this exercise, you can say something about it or write down your experience:

- What did you feel and think when you saw your Little Me?
- What did your Little Me need from you?
- What did you want to say to your Little Me, or give to him or her? Was it an object (for example a cuddly toy) or a supportive message?

Note: You can also adapt this exercise. You can go back to another situation where things were always nice, for instance with grandparents or others. Or you can visit your Little Me at school. You can also meet people who played an important role at the time (parents, brothers, sisters, classmates, teachers).

If this exercise goes well, you can decide by yourself or together with your therapist to direct the visualisation exercise at unpleasant situations in the past and present. When you do this, the first thing is to get a good picture of a difficult situation from your past that contributed to your modes forming. To do this, first you can call up an unpleasant situation from the present in your imagination, or you can go directly to a difficult situation from the past. Secondly, there is intervention in unpleasant situations, and thirdly, comforting the vulnerable child.

Exercise 5.3

Back to past

*Part 1: Visualising an unpleasant situation
from the past*

The objective of this exercise is to use the unpleasant feeling in the present to go back to a bad experience in your childhood.

1. This exercise works best with your eyes closed, which enables you to concentrate better. But if that's too scary, you can also do it with your eyes open. In that case, gaze at a fixed point, for example on the floor.

2. In your imagination, go back to an unpleasant situation in the past week. Imagine it as if you were there again. Pay attention to what you see, to sounds, to smells and other sensory impressions. Go through what happens again. What do you see now? Who is doing what? What are you doing? What feeling are you getting now? What do you feel in your body? What are you thinking? If the unpleasant feeling is quite strong, stop the image.

3. Hold on to this feeling. Do you recognise this feeling? Have you ever felt this way before? Let the image from last week fade away, but hold on to the unpleasant feeling.

4. Hold on to the unpleasant feeling from last week and go back to your childhood. Wait until a situation from your childhood comes to mind where you also had that unpleasant feeling. You don't have to actively think of a very similar situation. A memory might pop up unexpectedly. If a memory doesn't come easily, just take your time.

5. Once the situation from your childhood has come to mind, imagine it as if you were there again now. About how old are you? Pay attention to what you see, hear, smell and so on. Go through what happens again. What is happening now? Who is doing what? What are you doing? What feeling are you getting now? What do you feel in your body? What do you think about yourself and others? When does the feeling get stronger?

6. Check what you need now (what basic needs were not met)? Is there anyone who can help you?

If you go directly back to the past in your visualisation, without a link to a recent event, start at point 5. You then immediately try to imagine that unpleasant situation vividly.

Note: It is not important that your memory is exactly accurate. It's about what you remember, how you experienced it and what conclusions you drew as a child at the time.

Part 2: Intervening in the unpleasant situation

The moment you find that the situation from your childhood is clear enough and the feeling is strong, but you don't know what to do, it is time to intervene in that unpleasant situation to help your Little Me. Perhaps Sarah's healthy adult will manage to intervene on her own. Sometimes you can also imagine someone else coming to help you, such as your favourite aunt or a good friend. Whoever steps in for you, you imagine what this helper does and says when he or she steps into the picture to support you.

If you're in therapy, you probably aren't able to think of how to fulfil your needs for yourself yet at this stage. That's why your therapist will come into that past situation to help. She will indicate that she is stepping into the picture to come help you, and she will do whatever it takes to protect your vulnerable child or Little Me. She stops the person treating you badly and comforts you or removes you from the situation. In other words, the therapist does whatever is needed to keep you safe and supported.

In this way, the therapist tries to fulfil the need now that was not met at the time, giving that situation a different meaning and emotional charge. For example, if you as a six-year-old are being bullied and the therapist sends the bullies away, you already feel a little bit better. When the therapist then brings in the teacher to prevent this happening again, your vulnerable child begins to feel protected and comforted. And this will also make you understand that you were not a stupid child, but that the bullies were mean and were not corrected by the teacher or your parents at the time.

The therapist will keep going until you feel good. If you see in the visualisation exercise that the person who did something to you (for example your parent, coach, teacher or bully) cannot be influenced by the therapist, it is usually best for the therapist to send that person away.

The way the therapist intervenes depends on the seriousness of the situation. In Nora's case, she has to intervene forcefully more often to prevent Little Nora being abused. She might even decide to lock up her father in prison forever or send him away to a desert island far from here. Things are possible in visualisation exercises that are not possible in reality. For example, your therapist can become much stronger or magically send people to the moon, which connects with the child's imagination. Anything is permissible, as long as that fantasy matches what the child needs to finally satisfy past needs. At first, it might be a bit strange to have something happen in your imagination that cannot happen in real life, but scientific research has shown that this has a real effects on your pitfalls and modes.

Part 3: Comforting the vulnerable child

After the danger has passed, the therapist pays attention to the vulnerable child. She tells the child in a calm tone what she said to the father and why. At the same time, she tries to comfort and reassure the child. Then the therapist will take the child to another place where it is safe, and you will do something nice that is age appropriate. With this, she activates the happy child.

Next, we look at how this exercise went when Nora first started working with it in therapy.

Back to the past with Nora

Nora says she was completely upset due a conflict with Frank over a broken teapot. She still feels very stupid and clumsy. During the visualisation exercise, she uses that unpleasant situation in the present to go back to the past and suddenly sees her father in front of her who starts swearing at her after she has fallen with her bike. She was eight at the time. The therapist asks her to describe that situation as if she were experiencing it now.

N: We're standing in front of the house. I fell really hard and my knee is bleeding. He looks at my bike and sees that the wheel is bent. He is furious and starts shouting and cursing at me. He asks how I could have been so stupid to fall.

T: How do you feel?

N: (starts trembling) Very scared. He says it's my fault. I've hurt myself very badly, but I'm too afraid to say it.

The therapist decides this is the moment to intervene.

What an aggressive reaction from your father. I'll come to help you and stand between you and your father. I'm going to say something to your father: 'Sir, stop yelling at Nora. See how your child is doing first, instead of worrying about that bike'. Nora, what does your father answer back?

N: He only gets angrier and steps up to you threateningly.
     He says: 'Why are you sticking your nose in?'
T: 'I've come to protect Nora from your aggression. She's not stupid, but got unlucky and hurt herself'.
N: He doesn't listen and looks at you very angrily.
T: 'Don't you dare come any closer, because I can take you.
     If you can't control yourself, you'd better leave'.
N: (scared) He's not going away.
T: OK, then I'll tie him to the lamppost and call the police … Look, the police are already there, taking him away. What's it like for you to see them take him?
N: (surprised and relieved) Is he really gone?
T: Yes, and he's not coming back for now. But how are you, little girl? Hard luck that you fell. Have you hurt yourself?
N: Yes, and my knee is bleeding.
T: Come here. I put a bandage around your knee and put an arm around you. You must have been so frightened. You can't help it if you fell! That bike can be fixed, mind you. We'll just take care of you first. Shall we go inside? Where shall we go?
N: (nods and seems a bit calmer) To my room.
T: Then I immediately bring chocolate milk and biscuits, to recover a bit.

Through this visualisation exercise, it becomes clear to Nora that she was always punished when something unpleasant happened to her. Because of this, she often feels unsafe and deficient. A punitive voice has formed in the back of her mind which is always getting angry at her when something goes wrong and says she is stupid and ugly. The fact that Frank has a short fuse and lashes out at her at the slightest thing only reinforces that voice. Nora has to get used to the fact that her therapist does not get angry at all, but instead cares for and comforts her. Note that the therapist does not physically put an arm around her, but in Nora's imagination as an eight-year-old child.

The idea is to look for people in your present life who meet your needs for contact, attention and appreciation. Sometimes that means reducing contact with people who don't, and having to look for new connections or sometimes even a different job.

Role-play

Instead of using visualisation to go to the past, you can also re-enact a situation from the past with role-play. Situations that occurred repeatedly and caused modes to emerge, but were not violent are particularly suitable to deal with in role-play. This kind of role-play consists of three parts in which you and the therapist take turns playing the role of you as a child or one of your parents (or another person). That provides a lot of information about how you felt as a child when your father or mother acted that way towards you. In part, it also provides new information about why your parent reacted the way they did at the time. In the three-part role-play below, we use the mother as an example, but it could be any other relevant person. If more than one person was involved in the situation, you might consider asking one or more additional people to take part in the role-play. This could be one of the therapist's colleagues, or a friend of yours who knows you well and wants to help you this way. In most cases, it is sufficient to only play the main person. You can also use the 'Role-play Worksheet' (Appendix 5).

Exercise 5.4

Role-play about the past

Part 1

Before you start the role-play, you will work with the therapist to consider what situation(s) often occurred that caused you to develop one of your pitfalls.

Role-play

In the therapy room, you re-enact a situation from your childhood that you found very unpleasant, difficult or frightening at the time. This means that you and the therapist do not stay in your chairs where you normally sit. You play the child you were then, and the therapist plays your mother.

Review

Afterwards, you sit back in the chairs where you first sat and discuss what you thought of that situation as a child then, what you thought about yourself and what you thought your mother thought of you.

Part 2

Role-play

Now you re-enact the same situation, but the roles are reversed. The therapist plays you, and you play your mother. You try to imagine why your mother acted that way using the information you now have about your mother at that time. For example, perhaps she couldn't cope with caring for the children and was often ill back then.

Review

Afterwards, you discuss again how you view that situation as your mother and as your mother, what you think about you as a child. In this way, you often discover that you were not the problem, but your mother was. She had many problems because of which you didn't get what you needed. Perhaps you understand your mother's behaviour a little better, but that doesn't mean that her approach can be justified. As a child, it caused you to suffer a lot.

Part 3

Role-play
Now that you see the situation differently, you can probably think of what you needed and what you would have wanted to do or say as a child in that situation. You switch roles again: you play yourself as a child again and the therapist is your mother. You use the knowledge you have now to think of what need was not met in that situation. Now you will do something with that. This will be something you couldn't do or say at the time, for example because it was too complex for you or because you were timid. Of course, that doesn't mean you did it 'wrong' back then. You didn't know any better.

Review
Afterwards, you will discuss what conclusion you can draw about yourself and your mother now. Do you have a better understanding of why that situation was so difficult, which basic needs were not fulfilled and what coping modes you developed as a result? Do you now see that it was not you but a parent who was deficient – and therefore that your conclusion that you were a bad, stupid or lazy child isn't right?

This role-play in three parts is not an exercise to learn new skills, but to get a different perspective on past situations. From that new perspective, you can adjust your conclusions about yourself or others. In Part 2, you discover the other person's perspective and in Part 3 you try a different response. Notice what this shows: you can deal with the pitfalls and modes created in your childhood in a different way.

Role-play about the past with Martin

T: Broadly explains the exercise first.

Part 1

T: Today I want to work with you to investigate when you started thinking that you can't do anything. Do you have an example from the past?

M: Yes, I was about 10 and had been cooking, but the potatoes were burnt. My mother heaved a deep sigh and said she would do it again herself.

T: I suggest we re-enact that situation. I'll play your mother and you play yourself.
       (T. stands up and asks Martin what the kitchen looks like. They use the furniture and objects in the room to imitate the kitchen.)
       We'll pretend this is the kitchen and you are cooking there. Come and stand here. Can you tell me something about your mother so I can play her?

M: My mother was always tired. That day, I think she'd been to the hospital with my sister again, and she'd asked me to cook. When she came in, the potatoes had just burnt.

T: That's clear, so let's start. You're 10 years old and are cooking, and I come in.

Role-play

T: What are you doing?! The potatoes are burning (deep sigh). Never mind, I'll take over. Anyway, you can't do it.

M: (falls silent and walks away with bowed head)

T: Okay, stop there. Let's sit down again and review this.

Review

T: That certainly was an unpleasant situation. What were you thinking just now when you walked away?

M: I just can't do anything. I'm a disappointment to my mother. I'm a failure.

T: And what do you think your mother was thinking?

M: Same thing: that I can't do anything and always do everything wrong.

T: Let's reverse the roles, to explore your mother's role in that situation. Now you play your mother and I'll play you. You are 10, so your mother is somewhere in her late 30s. She has many concerns about your sister and can't handle the family with three children very well. Now I'll be standing cooking. (Walks back to where the kitchen is.)

Part 2

T: Let's start, you're your mother and you come in and see that the potatoes are burnt.

Role-play

M: (sighs) What are you doing? How could you let the
      potatoes burn? You can't do anything anyway. Just let
      me do it again. (Sighs again.)
T: (falls silent and walks away with bowed head)
      Okay, stop there. Let's sit down again.

Review

T: Well played! So you were your mother for a bit. Stay
      in that role a little longer because I'm going to ask
      you a few questions about it first. What did you think
      when you saw that Martin had burned the potatoes?
M: Not that much. I was really very tired and didn't feel
      like taking over the cooking, but I had to.
T: What did you think about Martin?
M: I did feel a bit guilty that I'd asked him to cook even
      though he's only 10 years old. But then again, I can't
      really handle it, with all these problems.
T: So you didn't think: Martin can't do anything?

M: No, not really. I did understand that it was difficult for him.

T: Now step completely out of the role of your mother and take a look at the situation. What do you think about yourself now?

M: It's true that I wasn't very good at it yet, but I was also only 10 years old.

T: But at the time you thought: I just can't do anything. Now it looks more like your mother actually asked you to do something too difficult. What does that mean to you?

M: Maybe I shouldn't actually have expected to be able to do that then because it was never properly explained to me.

T: With what you know now, let's see what you would want to say to your mother.

M: That I can't do it yet, because I've only done it once with her and I don't actually remember exactly how to do it.

T: Fine, let's try that out. You play Little Martin again, but you say something with the knowledge you have now and with the awareness of what you need. I'm playing your mother again. (Walks ahead to where the kitchen is.)

Part 3

T: Let's begin. You're 10 years old and are cooking. I'm playing your mother again.

Role-play

T: (enters) What are you doing now? (deep sigh) How could you let the potatoes burn? Never mind, I'll take over. Anyway, you can't do it.

M: Yes but I can't help it, I've only done it with you once before.

T: (sighs) That's true, but I'm already so tired and I was hoping you could do it. Okay, stop there. Let's sit down again.

Review

T: So, you did that well, by saying something back this time. What was it like to do that?

M: Kind of crazy, but good. But I wouldn't have dared to do that before.

T: No, it wasn't normal in your home to answer back to your parents, but in this case, in hindsight, it was quite justified. If we look again at that statement that you couldn't do anything, what do you think now?

M: I still kind of think that, but I'm starting to doubt whether it's true.

T: I think back then you never got to learn by trial and error what you can or can't do, because everything was immediately taken out of your hands and you were told you couldn't do it. You can do a lot more than you think.

Through this role-play, Martin discovers that, influenced by events like this, he has developed the pitfall of Failure, created by a deficit in autonomy, competence and identity. Through role-playing, he starts to realise that he did not get enough guidance to learn things and do them himself. Because he adapted to the situation at home as much as possible, avoided difficult situations and was often told he was incompetent, he subsequently developed a guilt-inducing mode (guilt) and the avoidant coping modes 'the Stupefier' and 'the Pleaser'. He has come to believe he can't do anything, which is why he frequently asks others for advice.

Role-play about the past allows you to discover what you lacked and what unwarranted conclusions you drew at the time. Because you also take a turn playing your parent in this role-play, you might find out that (possibly despite their best intentions) your parent handled it wrong, which meant that your basic needs were not met. In this example, in Part 3, his mother does make some admission that Martin is right, and Martin therefore does not get a negative reaction to what he dares to say to his mother. For people who had much more problematic parents, this is not as plausible. If you feel that the parent would become angry if you answered back to him or her, the therapist might decide to do a fourth role-play. You then replay the third part of the role-play again, but this time the therapist is no longer playing the mother, but a parent who does respond well. This is a bit like the intervention by the therapist in the previous visualisation exercise.

Working with chairs
Putting your modes on their own chair in the room clarifies which different modes you have. In Step 1, you already tried to discover the different modes using chairs and in Step 2 to recognise them in everyday situations. Now you engage with those modes in order to change them. The chair technique is ideally suited to silencing the critical parts and making the coping modes (avoidant coping mode and inversion coping mode) less necessary. If this succeeds, it will create more space for your vulnerable and/or happy child.

In this step of treatment, the therapist therefore engages with the modes that lead to you not doing what would actually be good for you. Which mode is predominant depends on the mode in which you begin the session. For example, this could be a coping mode one time and a critical mode another time. We start with the critical mode, and the approach for the coping modes is explained in detail in Chapter 6 (p. 161, 'Role-play about the recent past').

A critical mode will never help you fulfil your needs because it is very one-sided in attacking everything you do and picking on every detail. Of course, it is good to look at yourself critically sometimes, but not without any nuance. A healthy adult who takes a critical look at themselves sees both your good and your less-good sides. They encourage you to do something about those less-good sides without setting the bar far too high. The critical mode can't do that and makes you feel worse and worse. That's why you need to silence it.

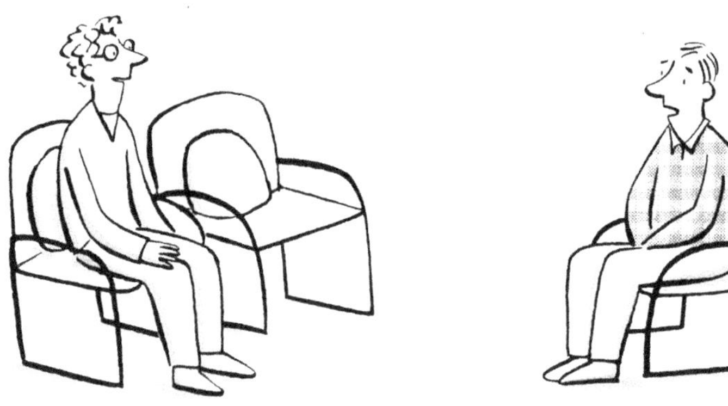

The therapist helps you to do this by first asking you to sit in the chair of the critical mode and to say what that part says about you. Then he asks you to come and sit next to him again and leave your critical mode in that chair. He then addresses the empty chair as if someone is sitting there saying all these negative things. If the critical mode is very much like one of your parents, he can also pretend to talk to that parent. Once in a while, he'll ask that mode to shut up. If it does not obey, he will continue until the mode is silenced. If that mode continues with negative criticism, he may even literally put that chair outside the room to make it clear that this voice is unwelcome in his therapy room.

Most people experience relief after completing an exercise like this. That critical voice is almost always present in the back of your mind and it feels good now that it is silent. You're glad there is someone who is on your side and sticks up for you. This allows you to connect with your real feelings and needs better. It does take some getting used to at first to see your therapist talking to an empty chair. However, you quickly get used to this once you realise that it works to eliminate the critical mode.

Changing modes using chairs with Martin

Martin complains that his mother has asked him to do something for her almost every day this week. The therapist decides to tackle Martin's guilt-inducing mode because his feeling of guilt is causing him to cross his boundaries time and again. Little Martin can't actually cope and gets so tired of everything demanded of him that he develops physical ailments.

T:　I hear that 'the Feeling of Guilt' is very active again because your mother is asking you to do something for her almost every day. And that while you also have a full-time job and barely get around to other things. Do you want to go sit again in the chair where we put 'the Feeling of Guilt' last time and say what it says to you?

M: I have to help her, though, because she doesn't have anyone else. If I don't help her, she'll get depressed.

T: Come sit next to me again and leave 'the Feeling of Guilt' in that chair. I'm going to say something to that mode. (Martin comes to sit next to him and the therapist talks to the empty chair.) I think Martin's Feeling of Guilt is completely exhausting him. It's not his fault that his mother gets depressed if he doesn't help her. She should get help from one of my colleagues for her depressive symptoms and not keep leaning on Martin. Then she can also learn how to do her own housework because she isn't disabled. (The therapist turns to Martin and asks what that mode says back.)

M: Yes, but my mother is afraid to ask others for help.

T: (to the empty chair) No, as long as Martin keeps helping his mother, she'll never ask anyone else for help. But now I'm here to teach Martin how to maintain his boundaries. There is no reason why his mother can't go and consult with the doctor about appropriate help. So I want 'the Feeling of Guilt' to shut up. Martin is not responsible his mother's happiness or unhappiness. (He turns to Martin and asks what that mode says back.)

M: Now that mode doesn't say anything.

T: (The therapist turns to Little Martin in the chair next to him.) Thank goodness he is quiet because I think it is really terrible that you feel responsible for other people's happiness much too often and don't do what is good for you. Little Martin deserves rest and space to do nice things for himself.

They then talk more about how Martin could handle this situation in the future and what he would like to do when he has more time for himself.

Changing modes using chairs with Sarah (without therapist)

Sarah is trying to change her modes on her own. She can use a chair for her demanding mode ('the Hustler') or her coping modes ('the Perfectionist' and 'the Stupefier'), but she also needs to put out chairs for Little Sarah (the vulnerable child) and Grown-Up Sarah (the healthy adult). After all, she is taking on the role of the healthy adult herself and has to act counter to those modes.

For example, when Sarah wants to rebut 'the Hustler', she puts two chairs opposite each other. First she takes the seat of 'the Hustler' and from there says what that mode thinks. For example, 'You always have to be the best version of yourself', 'Making mistakes is out of the question' and so on. She then sits in the chair opposite and contradicts 'the Hustler' (in the empty chair) from her healthy adult perspective. For example: 'I can't do everything perfectly. I also need rest and fun'. If 'the Hustler' protests, she sits back in that chair and says what he thinks. Then she goes back to the other chair as the healthy adult to come up with counterarguments. She keeps doing this until the demanding mode keeps silent, giving more space for Little Sarah.

She can do the same with a coping mode in the other chair. Engaging in discussion with a coping mode is a little different but broadly amounts to the same thing. We describe exactly how this works in the next chapter, which focuses on exercises to break your modes on your own (see 'Using chairs to change your modes on your own', p. 166).

Changing thoughts

Most negative thoughts are caused by the critical modes. For example, if you have a demanding mode, you immediately think that every little mistake is the end of the world. You should have known better and have to try harder from now on. Negative thoughts stemming from a mode can be changed by examining those thoughts and checking if they are correct.

When you focus on changing thoughts, first of all you try to discover the negative thoughts about yourself or others that often run through your head. The therapist then helps you refute those thoughts to weaken the modes that are behind them.

Self-inquiry circle
The self-inquiry circle is one way to change your thoughts. You can use this to take an unpleasant situation and map out the unhelpful thoughts and modes that play a role in it. Then you try to refute the original thought by examining what you actually need.

Exercise 5.5

Filling in a self-inquiry circle

The self-inquiry circle is completed in the following order. All the questions relate to the recent past situation that you have described. An example of a completed self-inquiry circle is given for Nora (Figure 5.1).

1. At the top, describe a situation when you didn't feel good. You can write it down the way you experienced it.
2. Follow the arrows to the right and fill in the boxes on the right:
   - What did I feel in my body? These are physical symptoms you felt in that situation, such as tightness in the chest or abdominal pain.
   - What did I think? Describe what you thought, both about yourself and about the other(s).
   - How did I feel? Describe what your emotions were in that situation (scared, angry, sad, etc.).

3. Follow the arrow to the bottom left and fill in the boxes on the left:
   - Which mode was this? What did he tell me? Fill this in if you recognise which mode was activated by this situation. Use your mode model as a tool to discover which mode (or modes) played a role. Then describe what that mode tells you.
   - What was actually going on? Describe the situation as an outsider looking at it, trying to describe the situation as objectively as possible.
   - What would you want to see happen? Think about what you would have liked to change about the situation so it would have gone better.
4. Follow the arrow to the centre of the circle and fill in the four boxes from top to bottom:
   - What did I actually need? Describe what basic needs you had in this situation.
   - What could I have done to get what I really needed? Describe how you could fulfil that basic need.
     - What did I do in that situation? Fill in what you actually did in that situation here.
     - What was the effect of what I did? Write down the effect of what you did. This is likely to be something that did not help and only made things worse.

When the circle is complete, you have probably discovered how your unhelpful modes led you astray, giving you the opposite of what you needed. By focusing on your needs, you can start to think about that situation in a more nuanced way and might react differently next time.

Appendix 2 contains the 'Self-inquiry circle worksheet' to fill in yourself. You can also download it from https://www.wiley.com/go/breakingnegativepatterns/1e.

At this stage of the change process, you are not yet expected to be able to complete all the parts without help. After all, you are not yet always aware that you are having unhelpful thoughts and don't know what mode they come from in all cases. Perhaps you can already start the circle yourself by describing the situation. Then write down what you feel in your body, and what your thoughts and feelings are. You then fill in the other parts of the circle together with your therapist.

In Nora's example (Figure 5.1), she discovers that under the influence of her punitive mode which she has named 'the Witch', she not only starts thinking very negatively about herself, but also does unhelpful things. This is compounded by 'the Tough Girl' taking over. By telling her friend that it doesn't matter and that she didn't feel like meeting up anyway, she makes everything worse. It means that her actual need for reassurance is not met and a new appointment is not made.

It is already quite difficult to describe a situation objectively because it is coloured by your interpretation. For instance, instead of 'My friend cancelled an appointment' in the first question, Nora could have answered: 'My friend didn't feel like making an appointment with me'. Only once you've completed the whole circle do you realise that she had a good reason for cancelling the appointment, and that she did not say she didn't feel like it at all.

Through her own reaction, influenced by the punitive mode ('the Witch') and her inversion coping mode ('the Tough Girl'), Nora inadvertently made things worse. She didn't immediately ask when they could reschedule. Of course, she didn't do this deliberately: her modes were activated without her realising it. Modes are patterns that have been part of your life for a long time and have in part become automatic and subconscious. By doing these kinds of self-inquiry circles, you become more and more aware of them.

If you want to work with the self-inquiry circle yourself, without a therapist, at first you might want to ask a friend to help look at it with you. When you put your mode model next to it, you'll usually discover which mode coloured your feelings, thoughts and behaviour. In the beginning, you probably also need help in formulating your need in that situation and how it can be met.

Figure 5.1   Nora's self-inquiry circle

You can also keep a thought journal to change your thoughts. Sometimes you can start doing that at this stage too, but if you are in therapy, a self-inquiry circle is usually somewhat easier to start with. Partly for this reason, I describe the thought journal in the fourth step (Chapter 6, p. 171).

Changing behaviour

In this third step, it is still not very easy to change your behaviour because in many cases your thoughts and feelings cause you to do things that don't help or even make everything worse. Even so, you can take small steps in this area by trying new things. Every time you don't immediately act from your old modes is a step in the right direction. In this section, we focus on strengthening the healthy adult and the happy child. Chapter 6 gives the steps you can take to change your behaviour when your healthy adult has become somewhat stronger in part through the exercises below.

Developing the healthy adult

Every time you notice one of your modes being activated, you are in fact already strengthening your healthy adult. If you think about the situation first and recognise your modes, and do not immediately act from your old modes, that's already a step in the right direction. It gives you a chance to try something new. It starts with thinking about what you actually need to fulfil your needs in a difficult situation. The fact that you still don't always know what you could ask of someone to achieve this is a topic you can discuss with your therapist. At first, you might be able to try new things with your therapist or with someone you know well and trust.

Learning to deal with the angry, enraged, defiant or sulking child

If you get too angry too often, it is best to start changing the underlying modes immediately. After all, this doesn't only cause you to suffer. People around you can suffer as well.

The sooner you detect that irritation is starting to build up, the sooner you can intervene. It is a good start to make an effort to detect your early signs of anger, irritation and so on. These feelings are often accompanied by physical signals such as gritted teeth, clenched fists and tension in your shoulders. Other signs are irritated thoughts, such as 'Oh no, what's going on now?', 'She obviously doesn't care' or 'He has no clue'.

Of course, you don't have to control your anger alone. Expressing your anger about what has been done to you in the present or the past can be a relief and gives you the energy to do something about it. But if you still find it difficult to express your anger like a healthy adult, it may be advisable to take a timeout for now. When you feel yourself getting angry, you can literally walk away or turn your attention to something else for a while, for example by looking at something else.

Chapter 6 explains how you can learn to express your anger better. There we also describe how people who express their anger too little rather than too much can learn how to handle anger.

Limiting the impulsive, undisciplined or spoilt child
You can only start restricting the impulsive, undisciplined or spoilt child after you realise that this behaviour gets you into trouble (for example debts due to too many impulse purchases) and is annoying to most people (for example if you impose your will). At first, you might not feel that bad in this mode. After all, you are doing what you feel like doing and satisfying your short-term needs. It is the longer-term negative consequences or reactions of other people that make you realise you are crossing a line.

Unfortunately, it is not easy to unlearn this behaviour. That is why it is important that you set realistic goals. To do this, it helps to enlist the help of other people who will point out if you go wrong again and also compliment you when you have achieved a goal. Of course, if you succeed in limiting your behaviour, you can also reward yourself for that.

If you are in therapy, the therapist can use a visualisation exercise to help you discover the influence your caregivers had on these modes. You can also use chairs to get to know the modes and to clarify why this way of responding will not ultimately help you move forward.

Giving the happy child much more space

The best way to empower your happy child is by discovering what makes you happy first. This is different for everyone, which is why you can start with a visualisation exercise in which you look for enjoyable moments in your life.

Exercise 5.6

Connecting with your happy child

1. Find a place where you can lie or sit relaxed and won't be disturbed for the time being. Take a few even breaths. Close your eyes.
2. In your imagination, go back to a pleasant moment in your childhood or more recently. This could be anything, such as a holiday, a good concert, visiting friends and so on. The most important thing is that you feel good there.
3. Try to imagine really being there. What do you see, hear and smell? Are you alone or with someone? Or perhaps a pet is keeping you company? How do you feel that in your body?
4. Concentrate on your positive feelings in that situation.
5. Examine what makes this situation so enjoyable for you. For example, do you feel safe and connected? Or do you feel free? Or do you feel relaxed?
6. Concentrate on this good feeling and your memories of what you liked to do in the past. Next, try to think of what enjoyable things you could do in your current life.

Through this exercise, you connect with your happy child. This is much more difficult or even impossible if you are in a critical mode or a coping mode. That is why those modes should be diminished as much as possible so you feel the space to do relaxing, fun things.

Homework

Observe situations in which you start feeling worse and start thinking negatively about yourself. Then try to identify the mode. Your mode model can help you with this. Most likely, a critical mode is active first and you start feeling worse and worse as a result. Also be alert to situations in which you find yourself feeling almost nothing or, conversely, overreacting. One or more coping modes are probably active. It is also relevant to analyse situations in which others treat you badly and take a close look at how you react to them. When you discuss these situations with your therapist, they will help you translate this situation into modes in which you keep getting stuck. The therapist might not only ask you to write down a number of situations, but also to start on a self-inquiry circle. However, you aren't expected to be able to make major changes on your own yet; it is still too early for that. First just try to understand how everything works based on your mode model. At the beginning of this third step, the therapist has also recommended that you should read this Chapter 5 as homework before you start practising.

Difficult moments

When you start changing your modes, you start understanding yourself better and sometimes you already feel somewhat better. But there will also be times when you wonder what you've gotten yourself into. You not only start looking at yourself differently, but also at the people around you. They are by no means always aware that you are changing and don't necessarily react positively. Because of this, it might make sense to ask your partner or someone else close to you to come see your therapist with you one time so they understand what you're doing.

You will sometimes also notice that you're actually afraid to change not only because others might react negatively but also because, aside from being problematic, your modes are also familiar. Most people don't really like change, even if it is actually better for them. Even people who don't have severe problems find it difficult to change their habits. Just look at people trying to adjust their diet, start exercising or find a different job.

It comes as no surprise that the old coping modes often rear their heads and stand in the way of change. During this third step, in which you start changing, this can make it that certain exercises just don't seem to work, no matter how hard you try. But it is not at all unusual that exercises don't always go smoothly yet. The most important thing is to persevere and examine what obstacles still stand in your way either on your own or with others. Above all, don't be too hard on yourself because you're just getting started!

Difficult moments when you start changing modes

Sarah is trying very hard to change her old modes, but sometimes she also gets completely fed up and falls back into watching TV all evening. When her husband says something about this, she reacts irritably and closes herself off from him.

When this leads to an argument once again, she puts the situation to her friend. She points out to her that watching too much TV and getting lost on the internet was precisely one of the reasons to start changing modes. They look at her mode model and see that Sarah usually does this when she feels bad because she feels she hasn't done something well, for example at work. Together, they make a self-inquiry circle about that issue.

Sarah discovers that when she feels she hasn't done something well, she could actually seek support from her husband instead of closing herself off from him. Retreating and going into the Detached Self-Soother by herself is her old familiar mode, but now she realises that this only makes the bad feeling worse. She decides to discuss this with her husband.

Martin participates in all the exercises the therapist introduces, but he is often unable to actually feel anything in them. The therapist doesn't understand what is going on because he's doing the exercise perfectly by the book. Suddenly he realises that Martin is used to adapting to others – and therefore to him as well. He obediently participates in the exercise, while feeling nothing because 'the Stupefier' activates immediately. This is so automatic that Martin doesn't realise it at all and sometimes the therapist doesn't either.

The therapist suggests trying putting 'the Stupefier' on a separate chair and engages him in a conversation about the pros and cons of this coping mode. This exercise shows that Martin is actually afraid of soon having to set boundaries with his mother or at work. He is afraid they'll think he is egoistic.

The result is that both the therapist and Martin notice much more quickly when 'the Stupefier' sabotages one of the exercises.

For **Nora** too, coping modes occasionally come into play when exercises don't go smoothly. She is very sensitive to criticism, so it happens quite often that a neutral or even friendly comment from the therapist is still interpreted as criticism by the punitive mode, 'the Witch'.

For example, this happens when confusion arises about the appointments. The therapist asks Nora if it is possible to make another appointment that week because she already has another appointment at the time they had agreed. Nora takes this as rejection, with 'the Witch' saying: 'If something goes wrong, it's your own fault'. Her coping mode becomes active almost automatically. So her tough mode says it doesn't matter and that she doesn't have time this week. For a while, the therapist doesn't realise that this is Nora's tough mode and agrees.

The next time Nora doesn't show up at all because by now another coping mode, 'the Wall', has taken over. The therapist looks at her mode model again and then realises she should have responded differently last week. She realises that she did not see at the time that it was Nora's tough mode that said she didn't need an appointment. She calls Nora and apologises for the mistake. She discusses with her which modes were unwittingly activated and convinces her to come back again.

* * *

Step 3 of changing modes contains various types of experiential exercises to get you started on changing your modes. At this stage, the therapist still has an active role in helping clients to change modes – and if you are working on them independently, it is still very helpful to have a friend's support.

Step 3 Overview summarises the elements of Step 3.

In Chapter 6, Step 4, you will learn how to gain a better grip on your modes and how to develop your healthy adult and happy child further. The role of the therapist or your friend then gradually changes.

Step 3 Overview

Starting to change modes (usually takes 18–28 weeks)

Section	Therapist	Client	You do it yourself	Friend
Recognising modes	Helps recognise modes using the mode model.	Begins to recognise modes from time to time, but does not yet feel able to do anything with them.	You are able to recognise modes better and better.	Is getting better at recognising the influence of modes on contact with other people.
Setting goals in changing modes	Gives explanation about the method in the third step of the treatment.	Reads Chapter 5.	You read Chapter 5.	Reads Chapter 5.
Changing modes with experiential exercises	Actively intervenes in: • visualisation exercise • role-play • chair exercise.	The visualisation exercise, role-play and chair exercise bring up a lot. Begins to recognise what role caregivers and others played in modes that have formed.	You try the visualisation exercise. You do the chair exercise, with your own healthy adult intervening and supporting the child.	Listens and shows understanding. Doesn't judge too quickly and focuses on asking about feelings.
Changing modes by changing thoughts	Helps fill in the self-inquiry circle.	Can fill in part of the self-inquiry circle.	You use the self-inquiry circle and maintain a thought journal.	Listens and shows understanding. Doesn't judge too quickly and focuses on asking about feelings.

Starting to change modes (usually takes 18–28 weeks)

Section	Therapist	Client	You do it yourself	Friend
Changing modes by changing behaviour	Does not expect immediate change in client behaviour yet.	Cannot change much in their behaviour yet, but has a growing understanding of how their behaviour is determined by their modes.	You are already trying something out and noticing the effect.	Gives you compliments when you try something out.
Homework	Suggests simple homework assignments.	Sometimes succeeds, but often not.	You make a list of what you want to try out.	Discusses with you how the homework is going.
Difficult moments	Sometimes fails to realise that certain modes get in the way of change.	Drops out if he or she finds the therapist too critical. Or still doesn't do much with what he or she has learnt.	You find that old modes are persistent when you are stressed.	Sees that you sometimes fall back into old modes.
Tips for difficult moments	As soon as something seems to go wrong, investigates which modes are likely to be responsible for this. Explains what she believes activates those modes.	Tries to continue therapy and, if possible, discusses what she does not like about the therapist or the therapy.	You react mildly and uncritically to the tendency to fall back into old modes.	

6

Step 4: Changing your modes independently

In this step, you learn to break your modes increasingly on your own. By now, you have a better understanding of how those modes formed in your childhood. You are also much better able to detect when certain pitfalls and modes are activated. In Step 4, you will discover that there are factors in your current life that perpetuate your old modes. If you are working on changing your modes on your own, you will already have done most of the exercises independently. If you have been working with a therapist, they will now encourage you to start changing your modes on your own, step by step. This step takes between 20 and 40 weeks.

Examples of insights into the influence of your modes

As you have a better understanding of how your modes influence your life, you can also start trying out new things.

Martin discovers that there are people who take advantage his helpfulness too much. This is the result of his mode 'the Pleaser'.

Sarah notices that it is convenient for some people at work that she always works so hard. This is influenced by her mode 'the Perfectionist'.

Nora realises that her boyfriend is not usually able to support her when she has difficulties. She discovers she has never said anything about it because she was in 'the Wall' mode.

Setting goals

The goals during this fourth step remain broadly the same as those in Step 3 (Chapter 5). The main differences are your own input as well as your therapist's role. This is because as your healthy adult develops, you can take over the role of your therapist. You have repeatedly heard what your therapist said to answer your critical mode, and now you try to do it yourself, in your own words. The therapist becomes more of a coach, guiding your healthy adult and letting you know how to change your modes independently.

What is important is that your healthy adult starts managing your unhelpful modes. An element of this is to recognise when which mode becomes active. This enables your healthy adult to intervene earlier in daily life and make sure that difficult situations don't get out of hand, or that you don't get overwhelmed by emotions. In other words, as a healthy adult yourself, you gradually learn to support your vulnerable child and express your anger and curb your impulsive, undisciplined or spoilt child mode. Also when the critical mode turns up, you realise it sooner, and you can increasingly silence it yourself. Your coping modes are now only activated when your healthy adult sees fit – meaning they are more attuned to the situation as it actually is. At the same time, there is more and more space for the happy child.

Behavioural change

Martin is going to try to say 'no' more often when other people want something from him.
Nora wants to be less tough and ask for help more often.
Sarah is going to lower the bar for herself.

You will now do the exercises to change your modes that you already know from Chapter 4 on your own. The focus here is more on behavioural change. Your basic needs are now being met better, you've already started thinking about yourself differently, and you also feel different. Now it is time to reap the benefits of that in practice, with or without the support of others. When you change your modes, you will behave differently. Other people around you will notice this as well and that isn't always easy for them. You are likely to face difficult choices in work or relationships. You might also distance yourself more from people who are not a good influence on you or even part company from them. This can even include your relationships with family members.

Effect on people around you

Martin notices that it is quite hard for certain friends who would always ask him for help to get used to him saying 'no' more often.
Nora notices that it isn't very easy for Frank that she expects different things of him.
Sarah stops taking work home. Her colleagues notice that now she doesn't always finish everything on time.

How does an appointment with your therapist go?

As we have mentioned, the therapist becomes more a coach who supports and encourages you. You indicate what you want to discuss and name the modes you have recognised. The therapist works with you to determine which exercise is best for you to do together. When doing this, she will encourage you to take over her role, especially in the experiential exercises. You use a self-inquiry circle or a thought journal to independently adjust your thoughts about situations. Sometimes this will work, but sometimes not quite yet. You will then ask the therapist for help.

The therapist increasingly emphasises the fact that you not only need to think differently, but also to act differently – both inside and outside the sessions. In sessions, for example you are already confident to express your opinion to the therapist without being afraid that she will disapprove of you. You will now try that outside therapy as well. The homework consists of practising new behaviours that help your basic needs to be met in your present life. This means that your behaviour becomes increasingly balanced:

- You express your feelings and opinions appropriately to the situation more often.
- You have self-confidence and your trust in others increases.
- You take on things independently.
- You don't only consider others, but also think of yourself.

- You take enough time for relaxation and are less hard on yourself.
- Your self-control improves.
- You treat other people respectfully and fairly.
- You see others as equal to yourself.
- You can handle unfair situations without constantly seeing yourself as a victim.
- You have an improving understanding of who you are and how the world works.

Changing modes in your own way

Experiential exercises in this step can focus on the past, the present and the future. The same goes for changing your thoughts. The experiential exercises and addressing unhelpful thoughts are already largely being done independently. However, behavioural change is still new at this stage of treatment, and you often still need support with this from your therapist or a friend.

Gaining new experiences

As you become more aware of which basic needs were not fulfilled in the past, you are more likely to recognise when you find yourself in a similar situation. There is a high chance that your old coping modes will become active in such situations, strengthening your old critical modes and child modes again. You can then try to decide how you will react if something like this happens to you again. To do this, it helps to ascertain why you unexpectedly fell back into your old coping mode in that situation. This can be done either with a visualisation exercise or using chairs. You can then try out new behaviours in a role-play.

**Visualisation exercise in which you intervene in
the past yourself**
The visualisation exercise changes because now you will intervene as a healthy adult yourself. An extra part will be added. First you make a connection between what happened recently and the

memory it evokes. Once you have done this, you are Little Me again for a while, experiencing what went wrong back then. Then you stop the image. The therapist suggests that instead of her, you come into the picture and intervene as your healthy adult (Grown-Up Me). Your healthy adult therefore steps into the picture and does whatever it takes to protect Little Me and stop the one who is behaving badly. Then, as a healthy adult, you comfort and support the vulnerable child. If this goes well, the therapist stops the image again for a moment in order to start the fourth part of the exercise. She will ask you to be Little Me again, experiencing how your healthy adult (Grown-Up Me) intervenes to provide protection and then comfort. This is best illustrated using an example.

Intervention by Martin's healthy adult

Martin had an experience this week that he would like to discuss. He had come up with a new way of archiving documents. His supervisor wouldn't even hear him out and cut him off. He said: 'We've always done it this way. Just stick to your own job'. Martin didn't dare to argue.

The therapist suggests a visualisation exercise and explains that Martin can try to intervene himself this time. In preparation, the therapist can first ask Martin to imagine what Grown-Up Martin looks like (see Exercise 6.7). Through this situation at work, Martin arrives at a memory of the past (see Chapter 3, 'Visualisation exercise to discover pitfalls and modes with Martin', p. 94). He wants to learn to play the piano, but his father rejects the idea.

Part 1

T: Visualise again how that went. How old are you?

M: I'm seven. I go to my father and ask him if I can take piano lessons. He says it's out of the question.

T: What do you do?

M: I say the piano is my favourite instrument. But he says all children should learn to play the recorder first. The music school said so and that's that. I know there is no point in pressing further because he turns around and goes back to reading the paper (sighs and looks sad).

Part 2

T: OK, just stop the image for a moment and go back to that moment when father says it's out of the question. Little Martin is clearly feeling disheartened and sad. Now I'll ask you to come in as Grown-Up Martin [GM]. What do you see and hear?

GM: I see my father looking very stern and not even hearing Martin out. Martin walks away disappointed.

T: What do you want to do about that?

GM: I say to my father: 'You need to listen to Martin, because he really does know which instrument he wants to play'.

T: What does your father say back?

GM: He stands firm and says that I don't know what's good for Martin.

T: Keep going. What do you want say to your father now? Be as clear as possible.

GM: Why are you so convinced of your opinion anyway? I'm sure the music school's rules aren't that strict. As far as I'm concerned, Martin can pursue what he likes. And then he'll also learn much better. When you do something you like, you practise more often.

T: Is your father quiet now?

GM: Yes, he stays quiet and walks away.

Part 3

T: Very good. Take another look at Little Martin. What do you see and what else do you want to do?

GM: He looks surprised but also relieved, and I say: 'You do get to choose which instrument you like best. You don't have to worry about your father stopping it anymore, because I'm going to help you. Come on, Martin. We'll go to the music school together to ask if they still have a place for you'.

Part 4

T: I think that Little Martin is very happy now. Just freeze the image for a moment. Now you're Little Martin again. Let's investigate how he feels when Grown-Up Martin intervenes. We'll rewind the picture a little but to the moment when Grown-Up Martin enters.

M: (nods)

T: Grown-Up Martin comes in and tells your father that he thinks he shouldn't be so strict, and that he thinks you should be able to start playing piano. What do you think of that?

M: Fine, but my father still looks angry.

T: Grown-Up Martin ignores that and is so clear to your father that he walks away. He says you do get to choose your own instrument, and takes you to the music school.

M: Yes, that's great.

T: Grown-Up Martin is sure to arrange it that your father can't interfere anymore.

M: That's a bit crazy, but I hope it works out.

After this exercise, the therapist and Martin conclude that the situation at work activated old pitfalls such as Subjugation and Failure and then 'the Pleaser' becomes active. Then they discuss the incident from last week. They conclude that Martin's idea wasn't bad at all. He might just be unlucky to have a supervisor who doesn't like change. In the future, he can consider saying something back when he realises that his old modes are wrong. If that has little effect, it's not because of his idea, but because of the other person. If he is repeatedly not taken seriously at work, perhaps he should consider looking for another job.

This example illustrates that Martin is able to switch perspectives. As Grown-Up Martin, he feels strong enough to stand up to his father. As Little Martin, he experiences that Grown-Up Martin supports him in making his own choices.

Sarah is a little further along in this phase and has her healthy adult intervene directly in situations she remembers from the past and then links that to the situation in the present that triggered it.

Intervention by Sarah's healthy adult

Sarah feels very stressed after something has gone wrong at work. While she doesn't have a very big part in, she still feels she could have prevented it.

Part 1
Through a visualisation exercise, Sarah comes to a situation in her childhood where she is helping her father mow the lawn. She is seven and accidentally pushes the lawnmower into a flower-bed. Her father immediately gets angry and

calls Sarah clumsy. He pulls the mower out of her hands. Sarah feels ashamed and thinks she has to try even harder from now on.

At that point, Sarah decides to let her healthy adult intervene. She steps into the picture as the Sarah she is now (Grown-Up Sarah) and starts talking to her father.

Part 2

GS: Stop being so critical. Sadie was enjoying helping you, but you can't expect a seven-year-old child to know exactly how to do it. If something goes wrong, it's not a disaster, is it? (She looks at her father and sees he is annoyed by what she says as Grown-Up Sarah)

Father: Sadie is always so clumsy. She needs to pay more attention!

GS: So you insist that everything should always be perfect and that every little mistake should immediately be severely punished? Sarah is only seven! Such a small child can't be expected to do that well at all yet. Working in the garden together should just be fun. So I disagree with you. No one is perfect, and by doing that you're only teaching Sarah that every little mistake is a disaster. This makes her very stressed about everything she does. Working in the garden with your father should be fun – not an exercise in perfection.

Part 3

GS: Come here Sarah, we'll leave your father here to do everything perfectly himself, and we'll have fun at the playground.

Together, they walk to a nearby playground, and Sarah visualises what it was like when she went out to have fun playing with her friends.

Through this visualisation exercise, it becomes clearer to Sarah that her basic need for spontaneity, play and relaxation was very often suppressed by her father's criticism. She heard her father's messages so often that now she constantly has a demanding voice in the back of her mind, magnifying every little mistake into a disaster. She resolves to contradict that demanding mode more often. Finally, Sarah draws conclusions about the difficult situation at work. She realises that she doesn't have to worry about that mistake. Not everything has to be perfect, and she isn't responsible for everything.

Future-oriented visualisation exercise

You can use visualisation exercises not only to change past situations, but also to try new things. You should choose situations in which you expect your pitfalls and modes to be activated again. For example, if you are afraid to express criticism or ask for help, think of a situation in the near future where you expect criticism. You resolve to address that situation from your healthy adult perspective.

In this way, Martin can try out what it is like to refuse something or express his opinion without being subservient ('the Pleaser'). Sarah can try asking for support instead of solving everything herself from 'the Perfectionist'. Nora sometimes finds it difficult to express criticism without quickly becoming very angry (Angry Nora) and at other times she tends to do this from her tough mode. She therefore chooses a situation where she wants to express criticism. Once you have chosen a situation to try out that new behaviour, make it as concrete as possible: when and where does the situation play out, and who is involved? Of course, you can't predict exactly how something will turn out in reality. Still, it helps if you try to imagine how your healthy adult would react, and you can avoid reacting from a pitfall or mode.

Future-oriented visualisation exercise with Nora

Nora thinks that she and her boyfriend Frank should divide the tasks around the house more fairly. He doesn't currently have a job and she works 20 hours a week. She decides it is best to discuss this with him at a quiet moment when they both have time. The therapist suggests doing a visualisation exercise to prepare for this conversation.

T: To prepare for this conversation, you might want to reflect on how your healthy adult discusses problems. Think back to that conversation with your friend the other day, about her rescheduling appointments so often. Just close your eyes for a moment and think about how you felt then.

N: That conversation actually did go very well. I felt sure of myself. I could calmly explain to her why it was so annoying to me. I sat up straight and looked her in the eye.

T: So that's how Grown-Up Nora feels and behaves when she discusses a problem. Hold on to this feeling and now imagine the conversation with Frank tomorrow night.

N: We're sitting on the sofa with a cup of coffee and I say I want to talk to him about how we divide chores in the household. I'm going to say that I think we should write down all the tasks and then agree on who is responsible for what.

T: Say it to him as if you were actually sitting next to him now.

N: Frank, I want to talk with you about how we divide up our household tasks. I suggest that we write down all the tasks and then agree on who's responsible for what.

T: Sounds good. What happens now?

N: Frank sighs deeply and says he doesn't feel like doing that. I actually want to get angry again because he does much less than I do. He takes advantage of the situation that I can't stand too much clutter, so I always clean up everything before he does.

T: OK, be careful that Angry Nora doesn't take over now because then it will probably get out of hand. Let Grown-Up Nora say that you really want to talk about it seriously and that you also value his opinion on dividing up the chores.

N: I really want to talk about this seriously, which is why I want to start with you by writing down what needs to be done in the house and how we divide it up now. You can also mention things that belong on the list. We'll only see if it's more or less evenly distributed after that.

T: Very good. What happens now?

N: He does calm down a bit, but still has a difficult look.

T: OK, let's stop now and discuss how it went. Just open your eyes again.

After this, Nora and the therapist discuss how Nora can make sure that she stays in her healthy adult mode as much as possible and avoids getting carried away by her child modes or coping modes. The therapist explains that of course she can't guarantee that Nora will succeed in agreeing on better division of tasks with Frank. It's about having the conversation from her healthy adult perspective. At least then the chances of success are higher.

If things do turn out differently in practice, then you can look at who or what was the reason for that. There is a high chance that it wasn't because of how you brought it up (from your healthy adult point of view), but due to factors within the other person or the circumstances. In the example above, Frank's unwillingness may be related to the fact that he has other problems, making him unable to have this conversation properly. Perhaps he has a few pitfalls of his own that play a role in this.

Role-play about the recent past

Role-playing about situations that happened recently can help you to better understand why misunderstandings or conflicts arise. The role-play we discuss here consists of three parts, as does the 'Role-play about the past' (see Exercise 5.4). This is about a recent situation. You can also use the role-play to prepare for future situations. Read more about this in Chapter 7.

Exercise 6.1

Role-play about the recent past

Part 1

You work with the therapist in the therapy room to re-enact a situation you recently experienced in which you felt scared, angry or sad. You play yourself and the therapist plays the other person involved in the situation. After you have re-enacted the situation, you discuss what you thought of the situation and what you thought about yourself and the other person. You try to understand why the situation went badly.

Part 2

Play the same situation again, but switch roles. The therapist plays you and you play the other person. You try to imagine why the other person acted the way they did, by putting yourself in their place. Afterwards, you discuss how you view the situation from the other person's perspective and what they think about you. In this way, you often discover not only the other person's part in this, but also what your own part was in the situation. The therapist can say something about how she experienced your behaviour. Perhaps you were too sharp (from your tough mode) or indeed too vague (by being submissive), and that evoked a strange or annoying reaction in the other person, making the situation worse. You might also discover problematic traits in the other person that you weren't really aware of before.

Part 3

Now that you see the situation differently, you can probably think of what you would want to do or say in that situation from your healthy adult perspective. The roles are reversed again, and now you play yourself again and the therapist plays the other person. However, this time you try to do or say something that you failed to do then, with the aim of fulfilling your needs as much as possible. If you resolve a misunderstanding or conflict in this way, this also fulfils the other person's needs better.

Review

After completing Part 3 of the exercise, discuss what conclusion you can now draw about yourself and the other person. With help from your therapist, you are likely to understand better why that situation led to a misunderstanding or conflict, and which basic needs were not met. You examine which of your modes played a role in this. It may lead you to try to discuss the misunderstanding or conflict with the other person again in the hope of resolving it. However, it can also lead to the realisation that the other person also has problematic behaviour and that you need to take other steps to address the problem. For example, it might be a good idea to use a mediator.

As with the visualisation exercise, you cannot predict whether the interaction will actually go that way in the future. What you can learn from this exercise, though, is how to address similar situations from your healthy adult perspective. You can see how that goes from the example of a role-play about Nora's recent past.

Role-play about the recent past with Nora

A few weeks ago, Nora managed to make new agreements with Frank about dividing up the tasks in the household. Today, she says she got into an argument with him after he reacted dismissively when she said he wasn't keeping to the agreements. The therapist suggests role-playing.

Part 1

T: I suggest we re-enact that situation to see what your role was and also to analyse his part. Where did the conversation take place?

N: On the sofa in the living room.

T: Then let's sit next to each other, and you start.
(They put two other chairs next to each other and sit down.)

N: Frank, I still want to talk with you again about how we divide up our household tasks. You never do what you promise.

T: Don't keep complaining about the household all the time. I do enough.

N: That's nonsense. It's 10 o'clock at night and the dishes are still there, and your mess is lying around all over the house. You just can't do anything.

T: OK, let's stop here.

The two sit back in their own chairs to discuss the first part of the role-play.

T: What stands out to you about this discussion? Do you understand which of your modes played a role here?

N: I think I started quite calmly. I made agreements with Frank a few weeks ago about how we divide tasks, but he hardly ever sticks to it. But maybe my tone was a bit from the tough mode.

T: To investigate that, now we'll reverse the roles. So I'll play you and you can experience how you come across to Frank.

Part 2

T: Frank, I still want to talk with you again about how we divide up our household tasks. You never do what you promise.

N: Don't keep complaining. I do enough.

T: That's nonsense. The dishes are still there, and your mess is lying around all over the house. You just can't do anything. OK, let's stop here.

The two sit back in their own chairs to discuss the second part of the role-play.

T: What stands out to you about this discussion? How did I come across in your role? How do you feel as Frank?

N: Actually, I thought you started well as Nora. But as Frank, I felt caught out because she's actually right. I don't like having this discussion and say that she just keeps complaining.

T: So you notice that Frank's strategy of 'offence is the best defence' immediately becomes active? And what do you do next?

N: I'm immediately triggered by that and switch to a counterattack.

T: Indeed. You started well, but you let yourself be tempted to counterattack, saying that he just can't do anything. What would you want to do differently from your healthy adult point of view if we reverse the roles in a moment?

N: Stay calm? But how? He really doesn't do what we agreed on!

T: You can say that, for example and then put more emphasis on how that affects you.

N: Well, I'm disappointed because I thought we'd made good agreements. But I'll try to say that.

Part 3

N: Frank, I still want to talk with you again about how we divide up our household tasks. You never do what you promise.

T: Don't keep complaining about the household all the time. I do enough.

N: I thought we'd made good agreements and I don't like the fact that you haven't kept to those agreements a few times already.

T: Yes, but I usually do. (Steps out of her role for a moment, leans towards Nora and encourages her to stay calm, to repeat the agreements again and stay with her feelings).

N: That's not true. I'm annoyed that you don't keep to our agreements most of the time. I'd rather have you keep to the agreements, and that you just check with me if you really can't manage to do the dishes one time.

T: (sighs) I'll try to do that, but I can't promise anything.

Both sit back in their own chairs to discuss the third part of the role-play.

T: How did you think it went now?

N: Better. In any case, it didn't turn into a fight. But it does make me a bit disheartened because I know when Frank says something like this it won't lead to anything.

T: It's true that we don't know if it will have an effect, but you did stay in your healthy adult and didn't let yourself be tempted to go on the attack from 'the Tough Girl'.
      If nothing comes of it in the end, you can discuss that with him again from your healthy adult point of view.

Using chairs to change your modes independently

In Chapter 5 ('Working with chairs', p. 129), we have already explained how to use chairs to discover and change modes. Martin and Nora got help with this from their therapist, and Sarah did it herself. Now the time has come for Martin and Nora to confront their critical mode or coping mode themselves too. The approach to these two types of modes differs slightly, so first we'll look at how Martin tackles his critical mode and then how Sarah handles her coping mode.

Exercise 6.2

Using chairs to send the critical mode away with Martin

Martin's 'Feeling of Guilt' is particularly active because his mother has asked him for help again, while he already has hardly any time to relax. The therapist suggests that Martin take a seat in the chair where 'the Feeling of Guilt' usually sits.

M: (The Feeling of Guilt:) I have to help my mother, though, because she doesn't have anyone else and if I don't help her, she'll get depressed.

T: Come back to your healthy adult's chair next to me and leave 'the Feeling of Guilt' behind. (Martin sits in the chair of the healthy adult.) I suggest that you try to argue with that mode yourself now. You've been feeling much more sure of yourself lately, and now you can try to be your healthy adult going against that mode.

The 'Feeling of Guilt' primarily formed under the influence of his mother, so Martin talks to the empty chair as if his mother is sitting there.

> M: I can't always help you, because I am also very busy with work.
>
> T: What does mum say now?
>
> M: That she doesn't have anyone else and can't manage it all alone. She also always says it in such a pitiful way that I'm afraid to refuse.
>
> T: Try going against it anyway. Now you know that help can be organised for her, but she's resistant to that.
>
> M: The doctor has already said that you should talk to a psychologist because the pills aren't helping enough.
>
> T: You've said that well. May I add to something that? (M. nods.) I think you've been leaning on Martin for far too long. His main responsibility is for his own happiness, and it's time for him to finally start working on that.
>
> After completing this exercise, they agree that the old modes are very strong, but that Martin is getting better at handling them because his healthy adult is getting stronger.

By doing this exercise a number of times, you will increasingly be able, with encouragement from your therapist, to silence your own critical mode yourself. This is not only in the sessions, but also in your daily life.

You can also work on your coping modes using a chair where you put that mode in, but you address it in a different way. The biggest difference is that you recognise that the mode did successfully protect you from unpleasant situations in the past. After all, a coping mode is formed in response to unmet basic needs in your childhood. You started avoiding or overcompensating to make that lack bearable. If you hadn't, you probably would have had a much harder time. But as we described in Chapter 2, today your coping modes often create unnecessary distance between you and other people. Even people who do have your best interests at heart and who could fulfil your basic needs do not see what you need because of your coping modes.

For example, if you don't show your feelings and are overly concerned with other people's well-being or if you avoid many situations, people don't really get to know you. The same happens if you don't show your feelings through inversion. For example, if you pretend to be completely independent while you are actually very insecure, people can start to think you are arrogant. Or if you always try to be the best in the class because 'the Perfectionist' is active, you might have difficulty making friends. And if you attack and deceive others, they will stay away from you altogether. In short, inversion keeps your vulnerable child out of the picture and you don't get what you need.

This is exactly why, despite the purpose they served in the past, now you have to ask the coping mode not to interfere. At the same time, you try to develop the healthy adult in a way that teaches you healthy coping modes. After giving your coping mode recognition for its service in the past, now you will still ask it to step aside. During the third step of the change, the therapist helped you do this, but in this fourth step you try this independently.

Using chairs to overcome a coping mode with Sarah

Sarah has taken on far too many extra tasks at work, while they are also remodelling the kitchen at home. She is in danger of burning out, but desperately tries to keep all the balls in the air. She notices that 'the Perfectionist' is working overtime again. Sarah therefore decides to enter into dialogue with that mode of herself. She takes two chairs: one for 'the Perfectionist' and one for her healthy adult. Firstly, she goes through the arguments of 'the Perfectionist' (P).

She then switches seats and counters those arguments herself from the position of the healthy adult (HA).

P: I can't give the tasks back now because I've already said yes. And who else should do it? The remodelling has nothing to do with it because we have a contractor.

HA: When I took on those tasks, I didn't realise that we were remodelling at the same time.

P: Yes, but who could take over those tasks, then?

HA: I know that I got used to only getting attention in the past when I performed well (recognition of the former function of 'the Perfectionist'). That's why 'the Perfectionist' is active again now. But that is no longer the case. What I need is more rest (recognition of Little Sarah's needs). I can speak with my colleagues about whether they can take over something from me. Perhaps a few things can also wait quite a bit longer.

P: You just have to push through because this remodelling will also pass. Besides, you don't have to do anything at home while they're doing that, do you?

HA: That remodelling needs quite a lot of attention. There are constant questions and unforeseen changes. It's quite stressful. So I don't have to do the building work, but I do have to help think about it, and that takes energy too. I hardly get around to doing the things I like anymore. So I'm going to write down all the things I'm doing now, and for each task see what I can delegate or postpone.

After this dialogue between 'the Perfectionist' and the healthy adult, Sarah realises that she doesn't always have to keep going, and that she's not alone. With this she can also think of ways to create more peace. She has good relationships with her colleagues, so they are sure to be willing to help her. She could also ask her husband to get a little more involved in the remodelling. In short, when Sarah puts aside 'the Perfectionist', she gains more relaxation and space.

You can also use chairs to learn to deal with the angry child modes or the impulsive, undisciplined or spoilt child. We describe how that works in Exercise 6.7.

Experiential exercises are important to change your modes in every step of your change process. They not only affect your feelings, but also your thoughts and behaviour. Conversely, different thoughts or behaviour can also make you feel better.

Changing thoughts

Thoughts can have a strong (negative) effect on your feelings and behaviour. In this phase of treatment, you increasingly do self-inquiry circles on your own. Now that you have a little more experience in recognising the modes and your needs in difficult situations, you can go quite far with this on your own (see Figure 5.1, p. 137). It is usually helpful to have your mode model at hand for this.

You will also start working with another method to explore your negative thoughts: the thought journal (see Appendix 3 in the back of the book). First you will use this to examine what thoughts came up in a difficult situation (under the influence of a critical mode or a coping mode) and then think of counterarguments from your healthy adult perspective. Exercise 6.7 shows you how to question your negative thoughts.

Exercise 6.3

Thought journal part 1: Mapping out the situation

In the first four lines of the thought journal, you describe what the difficult situation was, what you felt, what you thought and what you did.

Then you try to think of which modes became active in this situation. This is already a bit more difficult, but this is where your mode model comes in handy. It lists all your modes that may have played a role in this situation. Your healthy adult is now able to answer that question. If that doesn't work immediately, activate your healthy adult first (Exercise 6.6).

By naming which part of your reaction was justified, you acknowledge that it actually was a difficult situation, and that some of your feelings, thoughts and behaviour were a logical response to that. For example, if you have lost your way, it is natural to feel somewhat anxious and stressed. The thought 'I'm lost,' might be justified.

Identifying reactions that were too strong indicate that you were unable to think about the situation like a healthy adult. Thoughts like 'I'll never get out of this' and 'No one will go looking for me if I don't get back in time' are exaggerated in most cases. If you can't find your way because your plane has crashed into an immense jungle, these thoughts could be justifiable. But if you think this way during a walk in your neighbourhood, these thoughts are not helpful. Your thoughts and emotions were too strong in proportion to what was going on. Because of this, you were unable to think of a strategy to find your way back, but started walking around blindly, for example.

The last question, 'What did one (or more) of my modes do that made it worse?' refers to the extent to which your feelings, thoughts and behaviour got out of control under the influence of unhelpful modes. For example, you might panic in that situation (vulnerable or helpless child), start thinking you'll never get home again and run around like a headless chicken (coping mode).

Thought Journal Part 1

- Event (What happened and what provoked my reaction?)
- Feeling (How did I feel?)
- Thought (What did I think?)

- Behaviour (What did I do?)
- What mode/modes of mine played a role in this?
    1. Child mode:..
    2. Critical mode: ....
    3. Coping mode: ....
    4. Healthy adult mode: ....
    5. Happy child mode:..
- Which part of my response was justified?
- Which part of my response was too strong?
- What did one (or more) of my modes do that made it worse?
- What thoughts will I investigate?

(Appendix 3 gives the 'Thought Journal Worksheet'.)

By naming which part of your reaction was justified and which part of it was too strong, and therefore exaggerated, you begin to investigate your thoughts. You write down which thoughts you want to investigate and then go on to examine and change them. With this, you go against the modes that direct your thoughts in the wrong direction. For example, if you get lost, your critical mode might say 'You're hopeless!', preventing you from thinking calmly about how to find your way back. Or your coping mode (for example 'the Stupefier' or 'the Wall') whispers to you that you'd better just sit beneath a tree until you are found. You will start trying to change these kinds of negative thoughts into helpful or more realistic thoughts.

Examining thoughts is a skill that you need to learn. In Step 3 of treatment (Chapter 5), you still got a lot of help with this from your therapist. In this phase, you increasingly call on your own healthy adult (see also Exercise 6.7). Of course, the therapist will help you if you get stuck from time to time, but will mostly encourage you to answer the following questions about your thoughts yourself.

Exercise 6.4

Thought journal part 2: Thought investigation

You will be examining your thoughts one by one. For each thought, answer the questions below. You don't always have to use them all, and you can also come up with other questions.

Answer the following questions about your thoughts:

- What is the evidence for or against this thought?
- Suppose that a close friend went through this and thought this. What would I say to him or her?
- What would a close friend say if he or she heard me say this about myself?
- Do I think more negatively under the influence of my modes?
- Am I forgetting the positives?
- What is my part and what part do others play?
- Suppose that what I think is true, how bad is it?
- Can I do everything perfectly?
- What can I do myself?

Exercise 6.5

Thought journal part 3: Formulating alternative thoughts

After examining your thoughts and adjusting the influence of your negative thoughts, you can usually formulate alternative thoughts and think of how you could have handled this situation better. This usually leads to a new and better feeling. If, after examining your thoughts, the healthy adult concludes that you can do something, it is much easier to devise a strategy to get back on track. For example, you follow a stream until you get back to civilisation. This gives you a good feeling because you're going to do something to solve your problem. And eventually you find your way back because you were able to reflect on the situation.

- What would be a better way to look at it?
- What could I do better to resolve the problem?
- New feeling

Because you generally create a thought journal only after the situation is already over, you can no longer change that situation. But maybe you can do something to rectify what went wrong. And if something similar happens in the future, you might be able to take action at that moment. You then think back to the arguments against your negative thoughts. In time, this structurally changes your thought patterns and you start thinking from your healthy adult perspective more and more.

A thought journal by Nora

Part 1: Mapping out the situation

Event (What provoked my reaction?): Frank went cycling with his friends and didn't get home at the time I expected him.

Feeling (How did I feel?): Angry and panicky.

Thought (What did I think?): He isn't thinking about me. He doesn't think I'm important. Maybe he met a nice woman and has gone with her.

Behaviour (What did I do?): Texting and calling him the whole time. I couldn't concentrate on anything else anymore.

Which of my modes played a role in this?

1. *Child modes.*
   - *Vulnerable child.* Little Nora feels scared and helpless.
   - *Angry child.* Angry Nora blames Frank for abandoning her.
2. *Critical mode.* 'The Witch' tells me that he thinks I'm not important and is looking for someone else. It makes sense because I'm worthless anyway.
3. *Coping mode.* Seeking reassurance: texting and calling the whole time.
4. *Healthy adult mode.* Not present.
5. *Happy child mode.* Not present.

Which part of my response was justified? He almost never comes back this late, so I was right to be concerned.

Which reactions were too strong? I was completely panicked and furious and I kept on calling and texting him, while it was clear that he wasn't responding.

What did one of my modes do that made it worse? 'The Witch' made it worse by saying that he doesn't care about me, and Little Nora kept making it worse by completely panicking and not being able to do anything else.

Part 2: Thought investigation

What thoughts will I investigate? He isn't thinking about me. He doesn't think I'm important.

Answer the following questions about your thoughts:

- **What is the evidence for or against this thought?** For: Frank did not respond. Against: He often forgets to charge his phone, so he might not be able to respond. He could have a flat tyre.
- **Suppose that a close friend went through this and thought this. What would I say to him or her?** That her boyfriend isn't doing it on purpose and that there will be a good reason that he isn't responding.

- ***What would a close friend say if he or she heard me say this about myself?*** She would say that he does tend to forget the time when he's out cycling, but that does not mean he doesn't think I'm important. When he's out with the cycling club, he really won't be cheating on you.
- ***Do I think more negatively under the influence of my modes?*** Because I don't value myself and am so insecure, I get all sorts of things into my head.
- ***Am I forgetting the positives?*** X
- ***What is my part and what part do others play?*** My part is that I'd expected him home at a certain time, but he hadn't actually said what time he'd be home at all.
- ***Suppose that what I think is true, how bad is it?*** X
- ***Can I do everything perfectly?*** X
- ***What can I do myself?*** Stop trying to reach him. Call my friend for reassurance.

Part 3: Formulating alternative thoughts

- ***What would be a better way to look at it?*** He doesn't usually come back late, so there must be a good reason this time. He hadn't said what time he would get home anyway.
- ***What could I do better to resolve the problem?*** I'd be better off just doing something else that I enjoy. If he isn't here by dinner time, I can call one of his friends. From now on, I can ask him to say approximately what time he will be home so I can plan accordingly.
- ***New feeling.*** I feel less anxious and angry.

Completing the thought journal will help you put your thoughts into perspective. Everyone has negative thoughts when something goes against them from time to time. You don't have to put those thoughts completely out of your mind, but it helps if you can see the nuances so you don't fixate on the worst possible outcome. This usually helps you feel better too. And it also gives you the space to do something else, as a result of which the negative thoughts will not occupy you as much.

Changing behaviour

In this fourth step of changing modes, the focus is increasingly placed on changing your behaviour. If you discovered in the previous step that your opinion is important too, and now you believe it is okay to express it, the next step is to actually do that. It is difficult for anyone to change ingrained habits and automatic responses, but now that your critical mode is silent more often because you no longer align with it and ignore it, your automatic responses from your coping modes (the avoidant and inversion modes) are less necessary.

The healthy adult is a very important factor. He knows what healthy, balanced and sensible responses are. But sometimes you still don't know exactly how to do that in practice. You will therefore continue to build and deepen your healthy adult. It is equally important to be able to support and comfort your Little Me when needed. Finally, you have to learn to manage the angry child's anger, restrain the impulsive, undisciplined or spoilt child and empower the happy child.

Strengthening the healthy adult

You already have some experience with situations that you have handled well using your new experiences and insights. You did that from your healthy adult point of view. Every time you face a new situation where you expect difficulties, you can now prepare by calling up your healthy adult in your mind. You can use Exercise 6.6 to do that. You can then fill in the 'My Healthy Adult Mode' worksheet from *Breaking Negative Thinking Patterns* (downloadable from https://www.wiley.com/go/breakingnegative patterns/1e).

Exercise 6.6

Connecting with your healthy adult

1. Find a place where you can sit relaxed and won't be disturbed for the time being. Close your eyes.
2. Go back in your imagination to a moment in the recent past when you handled a difficult situation well from your healthy adult perspective.

3. Try to imagine you are the healthy adult again. What is your posture? How does your voice sound? What do you feel? What do you think? What do you do?
4. Hold on to this attitude and feeling and imagine yourself entering the situation you want to prepare for from this mode.

Another way to strengthen your healthy adult is to review what happened in a difficult situation afterwards from your healthy adult perspective. After describing the situation, make contact with your healthy adult (see Exercise 6.6) and determine how to deal with the situation in three steps (Exercise 6.7):

1. Acknowledge your feelings.
2. Contradict the negative thoughts.
3. Think about how you could handle it better.

You can also use this exercise for a future situation you are apprehensive about.

Exercise 6.7

Analysing a difficult situation from the healthy adult

To prepare, set up four chairs: one for your feelings, one for your negative thoughts and one for your behaviour all next to each other, and one for your healthy adult opposite.

This is a different way of using chairs than the exercises with chairs we have described before. So you put three chairs in a row and sit opposite them. With Nora and Martin, the therapist sits next to them and, where needed, helps the healthy adult take all those steps.

First of all, describe the situation you found difficult. Reflect on why it is so difficult for you. Then connect with your healthy adult (see Exercise 6.6). Go through the following three steps to determine how to deal with the situation:

1.   Acknowledge your feelings.
You can sit in the first chair for this, to concentrate on your feelings, but it is not necessary. Reflect on how you felt in the difficult situation. Then sit in the healthy adult's chair and, from your healthy adult perspective, tell the empty chair where your feelings are sitting that you understand why you felt this way. Acknowledge that the situation is complicated and painful or unpleasant for you. Against the background of your life history in which this kind of thing happened repeatedly, it is understandable.

2.   Contradict the negative thoughts.
If applicable, take a seat on the second chair (again, this is not mandatory). Your negative thoughts, which arose automatically in that situation, are seated there. These are messages from the critical modes, and sometimes from a coping mode, that hindered you from coming up with a good approach to the situation. Briefly repeat the thoughts that occurred to you at the time. Then sit in the healthy adult's seat and address the second, empty chair. Give arguments about why those punitive, demanding or guilt-inducing modes are wrong. They need to be stopped because they give you a bad feeling. If that works, you will actually no longer need the coping mode you would normally use. If appropriate, you can say why the coping mode is now unnecessary.

3.   Think about how you could handle it better.
In the third chair, say what you did from your coping mode in that situation. Because that was unhelpful, when you go back to the healthy adult's chair you think about how you could handle the situation differently. Ask yourself what you could do differently. The following questions may help with this:

•   What do I want?
•   What do I need?

- What can I do to achieve my goal?
- How do I also consider the other person in the process?

You then say to the third empty chair, where the coping mode is sitting, what you can start doing in such situations in the future.

Sarah's healthy adult analyses a difficult situation

A colleague of Sarah's, who she usually gets along with well, said something negative about a proposal she made in a meeting. She was quite upset by that. Sarah began to doubt whether the proposal was good enough and withdrew it. Afterwards, she decides to analyse this situation from her healthy adult point of view. She activates this perspective with the appropriate exercise. Then she sets up three chairs for the three steps to determine how to deal with the situation.

1. Acknowledge your feelings
   Sarah sits in the healthy adult's chair and addresses the chair where her feelings are sitting.

   S: You were shocked and also a little sad. I can certainly understand why. It's true that what Lisa did wasn't nice. You very often felt unsupported in your childhood, and now her behaviour feels like she is rejecting and abandoning you. It has also made you uncertain about whether it was a good proposal.

2. Contradict the negative thoughts
    Sarah stays sitting in the healthy adult's chair.

    S: 'The Hustler' says it wasn't good enough, but that's nonsense, because after that discussion there were also people who did think it was a good idea. Lisa was feeling a bit off that day. Perhaps she didn't realise she was hurting you by the way she was dismissive of your proposal. Just because she disagrees with you, doesn't mean you're alone. Some other people did react positively. You don't have to withdraw your proposal immediately.

3. Think about how you could handle it better
    Sarah stays sitting in the healthy adult's chair, but now makes her way to the chair of the coping modes.

    S: I immediately withdrew my proposal, but now I realise that I didn't have to. I'd better talk to Lisa and tell her what hurt me. Chances are we'll be able to talk it out. If she still doesn't agree, it isn't a disaster because others did think it was a good plan. My old pitfall that I always have to face things alone is not true. So I'm going to submit that proposal again anyway.

By taking the feeling seriously and disputing the unhelpful thoughts, Sarah is much better able to determine how to handle the situation.

Many people have a tendency to immediately start solving a problem in the second or third chair without first acknowledging their feelings in the first chair. When you start by acknowledging your feelings and not judging them, you create space for other thoughts and to think about what you would want to do differently.

Learning to care for the vulnerable child

Exercise 5.2 (p. 113) describes a visit to your Little Me in your imagination. But there are other ways that you have discovered when your vulnerable child is triggered. Maybe you disliked your Little Me in the beginning because you didn't understand his or her feelings. Now that you're on the fourth step in your change process, you have a much better understanding of where your vulnerable child's thoughts and feelings are coming from. Because of this, you no longer dislike Little Me, but sympathise with them. Your therapist has already shown you how to take care of your vulnerable child like a good parent, by comforting, supporting and encouraging them. Your own healthy adult will continue getting better at helping your vulnerable child. (And if you are breaking through your modes without therapy, with or without the help of a friend, you've already tried this.) You can try to hold on to that image of Grown-Up Me supporting Little Me by making a drawing of it, for example. Or you can select another symbol as a model for this. This could, for example be a song, a picture or a stuffed animal. You can use the 'My Vulnerable Child Mode' worksheet from *Breaking Negative Thinking Patterns* (available for download at https://www.wiley.com/go/breakingnegative patterns/1e.)

The needs of little Sarah, Martin and Nora

Little Sarah needs rest and the reassurance that she is doing well enough.
Little Martin needs more space to do what he himself wants.
Little Nora needs confirmation that she is worthwhile and belongs.

There are three basic components to caring for your vulnerable child. First, that you accept and allow your feelings. Second, that you consider what your vulnerable child needs now: what do you need right now? Third, that you do what is necessary to fulfil that need. This can be done in different ways.

One idea is to write a letter to your Little Me. In it, you start by showing compassion for your Little Me's feelings. Then make a connection to the past. Finally, you also say something positive about your good qualities.

Letter from Martin to Little Martin

Dear Little Martin,

You were not given much space to do what you wanted or liked in the past. I am here now to help you start doing that.

I do understand that it is very difficult for you to think of what you want for yourself, because you always think of others first. Your mother wasn't that strong, and had a lot of worries about your sister, so you automatically started taking care of

> *her. And you didn't dare to express your own opinion, because your father actually always decided what should happen.*
>
> *But now you are free to do and say what you want. I like seeing that you are getting into that more and more, and I will encourage you to do that as much as I can. You are a creative, active and caring man, and I'm confident that you'll keep getting better at that.*
>
> *Lots of love,*
> *Grown Up Martin*

Many people think they are taking good care of themselves if they have a healthy lifestyle and get enough sleep. They forget that you also need to pay attention to yourself at the emotional level. This means that you take your feelings seriously. If you are feeling bad, it is important to find out why, and whether you can do something about it. What do you need? How do you get support or understanding from yourself and from others?

If you feel bad very often, you might need to examine what is structurally wrong in your life. Is it your job, or your relationship, or something else? It might be good to change something about that over time. Should you look for a new job, or would it be a good idea to go into couples therapy?

It also helps to compliment yourself regularly. Especially if you have or had a critical mode, you probably haven't learnt to do that and aren't used to being proud of yourself when you've done something well. Giving the happy child more space is also an important form of self-care.

Learning a balanced way to express your anger

The idea is not that you never get angry again, but that you express your anger in a balanced way. In Chapter 5 (p. 102), we explained that you first need to learn to detect the early signs of your anger. In that case, it is about getting the angry, enraged, rebellious or sulking child under control. You can recognise these modes through physical signs and irritated thoughts. The sooner you detect that irritation is starting to build up, the sooner you can intervene.

If you feel yourself getting angry, the first thing you can do is to identify which basic need is not being met in that situation (see also Table 2.3 on p. 29). That makes it much easier to become aware of what is making you angry. It makes a significant difference whether it has something to do with not being seen, lack of autonomy, lack of self-expression or unfairness, for example.

When the angry child is triggered, there is usually also an underlying feeling of sadness, powerlessness or fear. Then you get angry because something has happened (again) that hurts you. If an impulsive, undisciplined or spoilt child mode becomes active, you will also be angry, but something else will be going on. (See section 'Limiting the impulsive, undisciplined or spoilt child', p. 195.)

If you are enraged, you might find it difficult to try the exercises in this chapter. In that case, it is best to do them several times after you were too angry and have calmed down somewhat. You might want to look at the 'My Angry Child Mode' worksheet, which you completed in Step 1 (Chapter 3, Discovering your own modes), to find out what your angry child looks like. You can also use this to identify which basic need was not met, and what is needed now. (The worksheet can be downloaded at https://www.wiley.com/go/breakingnegativepatterns/1e.)

Exercise 6.8 helps you discover where your anger comes from. Once you have discovered which basic needs were not being met in that moment, you can use that knowledge in Exercise 6.10 ('What to do if you get angry too quickly or too violently').

Exercise 6.8

Visualisation exercise to explore where your anger comes from

To find out why you found yourself acting from the angry child in a difficult situation, you can do a visualisation exercise as we have described in previous chapters. This time, the exercise is used to explore what caused you to lose control of your anger and what you would have needed to prevent it getting to that point. Do this exercise once you have calmed down a bit.

1. Find a place where you will not be disturbed. Close your eyes and imagine the situation when you got angry. Start from the moment when you were not very angry yet. Put yourself back into this situation completely, as if you were really there. Who is there with you, and what is happening? What are you doing and what are the others doing? What do you see, hear or smell? What do you feel and think? What do you feel in your body? Get to the moment when you notice you are really starting to get angry.

2. Concentrate on that angry feeling and release the image of that situation, or let it fade away. Hold on to that feeling and ask yourself whether you ever felt this way in your childhood. You don't have to actively search for a very similar situation. Maybe a memory will pop up unexpectedly. Just wait and see if a memory comes up while holding on to the feeling.

3. When a memory from your childhood comes to mind, try to visualise that situation as well as you can. You are probably still a child, so you are small and the others are big. What is happening? What do you see, hear or smell? What makes you angry? What do you feel and think? Do you only feel anger, or do you also have other feelings?

4. What would you want to see happen so you don't have to get so angry? Is there anyone who can help you?

5. Stop the exercise by opening your eyes.

6. Write down what you discovered. What is the connection between the situation when you got angry and the situation in the past? What is the theme? What made you angry (or scared or sad)? What did you think as a child? For example, did you feel deficient, abandoned, threatened or restricted? Were overly high demands set, or did you have a feeling of guilt? It could be anything. What basic needs were not met then, as a result of which you can get angry again now? In the recent situation, what would you have needed to stay calm?

You can use the chair technique to have the angry child speak with the healthy adult.

Exercise 6.9

Approaching the angry child with the chair technique

Set out two chairs: one for the angry child and one for the healthy adult. First, sitting in the angry child's chair, express all your anger. It is no problem if it's a bit too much, or too intense, because it can also be nice to let your anger out sometimes – in a safe environment at least. Then switch chairs. In the healthy adult's chair, you take a little more distance from your anger and try to look at it in a nuanced way. Point out to the child the advantages and disadvantages of letting your anger reign free in this way.

For example, the healthy adult might say it is best to start expressing your anger calmly because then the other person will usually listen better to the substance of your arguments. It is also important to learn to use this perspective to find words for why the other person's behaviour affects you so much. This could have to do with the other person's behaviour as well as your sensitivities. If you explain that, it is probably easier for the other person to understand why you are angry. The healthy adult can also try to empathise with why the other person did or said something. (For more arguments, see also point 4 of Exercise 6.10.)

After each argument by the healthy adult, switch places each time the angry child has a retort and give this side enough space to have its say. Then go back to the healthy adult's chair and reiterate one of the arguments you have just mentioned. Continue switching chairs until the angry child has calmed down.

If you are able to conduct the discussion between your angry child and the healthy adult in this way, you can also try to use this in future situations.

Nora uses the chair technique to learn to control her angry child

Nora is furious because Frank arranged to go away for a weekend with his group of friends without consulting her. The argument escalated, and they both said they might as well break up. The therapist suggests looking at this situation from the angry child and the healthy adult points of view. At this stage, Nora is already capable of playing both roles and takes on the discussion herself. In the dialogue below, AN stands for Angry Nora and GN for Grown-Up Nora.

AN: (in an angry tone) He never checks with me and now hasn't again. I'm sick of it. I think he's a self-centred bastard.

GN: I understand that you're angry. It is true that he didn't check with you. But by immediately getting

> furious and yelling, all you achieved is that he got angry too. It would have been better to say it calmly.
>
> AN: Yes, but I've had enough of him not taking me seriously.
>
> GN: Now you mention something that plays an important role. You don't feel that you are taken seriously. That's understandable, and it is all the more painful for you because you were also never taken seriously in the past. That is your bruise. Did you say something about that?
>
> AN: No, because he doesn't listen to me anyway.
>
> GN: Does it make him listen to you when you immediately start shouting? I think you're much more likely to get through to him if you start calmly at first. You know he's very sensitive to criticism, and if you're calm you'll be able to explain it better.
>
> AN: Yes, but what if he still doesn't listen?
>
> Grown-Up Nora falls silent and the therapist hints:
>
> T: You might say that you can always get angrier if he doesn't listen, but even then that it's still better to say that in a controlled way. For example: 'I have the feeling that you don't hear what I'm saying and because of that, once again, I don't feel taken seriously'.
>
> GN: OK, then I say that, but sometimes he just walks away. But then I can say that he can walk away now, but that I'll want to talk about it again later. Sometimes he needs to cool down before he can talk about this kind of thing.

Another way to regulate your angry child, but especially your impulsive, undisciplined or spoilt child mode, is to write down the pros and cons of this behaviour. These last three modes can actually be the result of a lack of boundaries in your childhood, leading you to develop the pitfalls Entitlement (grandiosity) or Lack of Self-Discipline/Self-Control. In this case, you might get angry because you don't get your way or others don't do what you want, or when there are tasks that you have to do.

In the short term, you don't usually realise that this gets you into trouble, but in the long term you might notice that people are afraid of you or start avoiding you. You are also likely to get into trouble because you neglect certain duties (for example filing your tax return). You often only find out that this behaviour is a problem if a friend, colleague or your partner takes the trouble to tell you that you are being selfish, coercive or spoilt in your behaviour. If they do this, don't be too quick to think it's because of the other person's hypersensitivity, but try to listen to this kind of signal. Investigate whether it contains a kernel of truth. One way to figure it out for yourself is to write down the pros and cons of these behaviours.

If the anger primarily stems from being wronged or treated badly and not having your basic needs met, then your irritation is entirely understandable. But even in that case, you have to learn to express your anger in such a way that your message actually comes across. There are several steps you need to take to express your anger appropriately. First, I describe how to handle anger if you don't have it under control that well and then, on the contrary, if you don't express it enough.

Exercise 6.10

What to do if you get angry too quickly or too violently

1. *Recognise early signs.* In Step 3 (p. 104) we have already explained the importance of noticing your anger early. You can do this by paying attention to physical signs and irritated thoughts. Physical signals could be that you get red-faced, clench your fists or your heartrate speeds up. The sooner you realise that something is irritating you, the sooner you can start on the next steps and take action.

2. *Count to 10.* If you unexpectedly get very angry, try counting to 10 before reacting. In other words, take a time-out to calm down and implement Step 3.

3. *Think about why you are angry.* You aren't just angry. Someone has probably done something that makes you feel misunderstood, abandoned or humiliated. If you get angry because you don't get your way, you need something else. Consider what you need, and from whom, to fulfil your need for recognition or understanding (see Exercise 6.8). If you have done a visualisation exercise before, you usually already know what your need is in this situation.

4. *Express your anger calmly.* If you know who and what you are angry at, you can say so calmly. Choose an appropriate moment for this. When you do this, remember to be as specific as possible about the other person's behaviour and why it bothers you. Avoid generalising language as much as possible, for example using words like 'always' and 'everywhere'. So not: 'You also always leave your mess lying around everywhere', but: 'I'm annoyed that you leave your shoes and coat in the living room instead of hanging them on the coat rack in the closet. I've asked you before, and you know I like the house to be tidy'. 'Why' questions can also lead to escalation, such as: 'Why do you keep doing that?" There is usually no intent behind it, so that question is unanswerable nine times out of 10.

5. *Put yourself in the other person's place.* If the other person probably didn't do something wrong or annoying on purpose, try to put yourself in the other person's place. That might already make you less angry.

6. *Intensifying anger step by step.* Get a little bit angrier if the other person doesn't listen or reacts negatively, but don't suddenly go from first gear into fifth. Try saying what irritates you again, but now with a little more emphasis. Also indicate that your need to be taken seriously is not currently being met.

7. *Insert a short break.* If your anger still flares up again, for example because the other person doesn't respond as you had hoped, take a short break first. For example, go and get something to drink or look at an object in the room or a detail of the other person (for example their hair or ears). Take a deep breath and think about what you want to achieve.

8. *Choose a calming symbol.* If you often find yourself in situations where your anger is triggered, you can also think of a calming symbol that you can use when you notice you're about to get angry. This can be an object (a stone or a picture) or something in your mind (a song or the face of someone who can soothe you).

9. *Get really angry if necessary.* If you find that someone is seriously overstepping your boundaries and your attempts to calmly say what you don't like have no effect, then of course it is okay to get a more vehemently angry. You probably still won't achieve what you want, but at least the other person will know that your limit has been reached. Please note that even then it is not advisable to go completely crazy.

What to do if you don't get angry or not enough
There are also people who do not actually express their anger enough. People usually find it difficult to suppress only one emotion (for example anger) and not others (joy, fear and sadness, for example), so suppressing anger affects all your feelings. If you are used to suppressing your anger, it can lead to physical symptoms or anxiety and despondence. In the long run, suppressing anger can even lead to increased blood pressure and/or depression. Look at these possible consequences as additional motivation to start learning to express your anger.

Exercise 6.11

What to do if you don't express your anger enough

To learn to express your anger in a healthy way, you can follow these steps:

1. *Recognise early signs.* Try to detect when you start to feel uncomfortable when something happens that you don't like or find irritating. Physical signs are important here, but not always obvious. For example, you may notice that you tighten your jaw, clench fists or start breathing faster. It is not actually that easy to recognise having irritated thoughts because you often suppress these thoughts without noticing or because they are mild: 'I don't really like this' or 'This isn't working out that well for me right now,' for example. Or perhaps you're angry with yourself while you're actually angry with someone else.

2. *Take these signs seriously.* If you recognise any of the signs mentioned above, try to identify what is bothering you. Who or what irritates you? Which need is not being met in this situation?

3. *Contradict negative thoughts about anger.* You might think that getting angry only has negative consequences. Your critical mode can think that you'll hurt others and then they won't like you anymore and will leave you. Your coping modes might say that you're better off avoiding conflict because you had very bad experiences with that in your childhood. It is usually necessary to nuance these thoughts and turn them into positive messages about anger.

4. *List the advantages of your anger.* Expressing anger gives you strength and energy to express your needs. The other person notices what is bothering you and

can do something with that. Sometimes others don't realise that their behaviour hurts you if you don't say anything about it. It can also help you set boundaries. Expressing anger can also be a relief and make room for other emotions that you previously suppressed.

5. *Express your anger (first in a safe environment).* It is best to start carefully. Always connect with your healthy adult first (see Exercise 6.6, p. 178) and then practise with people you trust, for example with your therapist. Remember that expressing your anger does not mean becoming aggressive, talking tough or snapping at someone. The healthy adult always expresses anger calmly first, for example saying, 'I don't like this very much,' or 'I'm annoyed by what you're doing now'. Only if that does not work can it be necessary to act more forcefully (see also Exercise 6.10 for this).

Limiting the impulsive, undisciplined or spoilt child

To illustrate setting boundaries for the impulsive, undisciplined or spoilt child, we use Frank, Nora's partner, as an example. Nora, Martin and Sarah do not have this mode.

Frank's impulsive, undisciplined and spoilt child mode

Frank has come with Nora to therapy a couple of times. Those conversations revealed that, among other things, Frank has the pitfalls of Failure, Entitlement (Grandiosity) and Lack of Self-Discipline/Self-Control. Because Nora and Frank argue a lot, the therapist asks Frank to describe the pros and cons of his behaviour. He does this using a number of situations in which he failed to honour the agreements about dividing up tasks at home:

Pros

I'd rather do something other than boring household chores.
I often get away with it because someone else will do the task.
From my spoilt mode, I can easily ignore that Nora is angry.
I'm very good at steering clear of tedious tasks.

Cons

I leave many things unattended to and then I don't solve my problems (for example no job).
That makes me feel like even more of a failure.
Over time, other people start to realise that they always do more than I do.
I run the risk that they won't want anything to do with me anymore.
My relationship suffers because I make Nora angry and sad.

When an impulsive, undisciplined or spoilt child mode becomes active, it is mostly others that suffer. Realistic limits were not set for you enough as a child, or you were even spoilt and now you get angry when you don't get your way. Actually, you were not only spoilt, but also neglected because your parents did not teach you to be considerate of other people enough or to handle setbacks. Your basic need for realistic limits and self-control was insufficiently met (see Table 2.1). This is sometimes also called a 'lack of frustration tolerance'. You might want to look at the 'My Impulsive, Undisciplined Or Spoiled Child Mode' worksheet from *Breaking Negative Thinking Patterns*, which you may already have filled in, to find out what your impulsive, undisciplined or spoilt child looks like. You can also use this to identify which basic need was not met and what is needed now (This worksheet can be downloaded at https://www.wiley.com/go/breakingnegativepatterns/1e).

It is not easy to limit these child modes because the very thing you are struggling with is a lack of realistic limits and self-control. At the same time, other modes may also influence the behaviour, such as the avoidant coping mode the 'Detached Self-Soother' or the inversion coping mode the 'Self-Aggrandiser'. These modes usually also need to change to make it possible to address child modes. With these coping modes, you do not initially realise that you have crossed a boundary. Most people only discover that they have a problem in this area through feedback from those around them (their partner or colleagues, or the police).

In the case of Frank, you can see that he only realised this when Nora said she had problems with his behaviour. You can only start working on a plan to change an impulsive, undisciplined or spoilt child mode, combined with one or more coping modes, once you recognise that you have these modes. You can try to deal with it yourself, and if not, your therapist can kindly but decisively teach you how to deal with limits and frustrations.

Exercise 6.12

What to do if you are impulsive, undisciplined or spoilt

1. *Recognise signs that others are annoyed with you.* It can be quite a challenge to learn to recognise signs that other people are annoyed with you. Most people won't say anything, but just avoid you. You can therefore assume that when people who have your best interests at heart criticise you, there is some truth to it. Ask them to explain their criticism instead of dismissing it.

2. *Listing pros and cons.* Start by noting the short-term and long-term pros and cons. The short-term benefits

Table 6.1   Listing pros and cons

	Pros		Cons	
	Short term	*Long term*	*Short term*	*Long term*
Impulsive child mode				
Undisciplined child mode				
Spoilt child mode				

will usually seem much greater than the long-term drawbacks. Have someone else look at it with you, especially to mention the drawbacks because you might only know or recognise some of them yourself.

3. *Fulfilling unfulfilled basic needs.* Next, use the information in Table 2.1 to investigate which basic needs are insufficiently met in your case. The main factor in these modes is a lack of realistic limits and self-control. You can use visualisation exercises here to help you figure out the role your caregivers played in the formation of these modes. Then, in your imagination, you can confront your parents for not setting realistic limits or not encouraging you to do boring, but necessary, tasks.

4. *Setting goals.* To fulfil the most important basic needs in the future, you need to learn to manage boundaries and be encouraged to do things that you find boring or annoying. First describe one or more goals as concretely as possible. You can determine what goals to set using the list of cons in the Table 6.1. Of course you won't reach your goal in one step, so break down your goals into achievable smaller goals. For example, if you want to start exercising, start with 15 minutes three times a week, then gradually make the sessions a bit longer to build it up to an hour each time.

5. *Reward for results*. When you succeed in achieving a sub-goal, you can give yourself a reward for keeping it up. For example, if you are working on learning to fill in your tax forms and clear the three-year backlog, it is best to plan to work on it for two hours on specific days and set a deadline in a few months' time. Give yourself a small reward after every two hours you work on that (a cup of coffee with some goodies) and a big reward at the end (a celebratory dinner).

The real reward, of course, is the relief of having sent those tax forms and knowing where you stand, so you won't keep getting more reminders. But that reward will only come months after you finish this project.

At the same time, don't be too hard on yourself if you don't manage every single time. The risk then is that you give up completely. Just go back to implementing your plan the next day.

Frank's small reward

Frank decides to make a plan for the days when he will do his household chores. He has discovered how soon 'not now' becomes 'never', so he starts by trying to do something that is boring to him, like cleaning, for half an hour every day. He starts with things he finds easy and give himself a small reward (half-hour of gaming) if he actually does it on the planned day.

Strengthening the happy child

You have already practised connecting with your happy child in Chapter 5. At this stage, you engage in more activities that reinforce the happy child. That means regularly thinking about whether you have enough time left over after work, caring for others and other commitments for relaxation and having fun. Some people don't even really remember what they enjoy because they stopped doing it early in their youth. For Martin, the problem is that he never actually discovered what he really likes because he always did what others wanted.

Because of this, the first thing is often to discover what you like. These can be activities that involve a time investment, such as joining a choir, taking a painting course or planting a garden. You can also do activities with people you like more often. Sometimes you have to combine that with making new friends. But many smaller things, such as those listed below, can also give you pleasure.

Giving the happy child more space

You can evoke the happy child when you. . .

> let yourself fall into a pile of autumn leaves
> sing a song at the top of your voice
> have a running race with children
> let the sun shine on your belly
> do a whole series of forward rolls
> go for a walk in the rain
> turn up the music really loud
> have a pillow fight
> play with water
> laugh at other people
> play with young animals
> hear the rustle of leaves
> eat something yummy
> play together with a ball
> build a blanket fort
> put way too many bubbles in the bath

All these kinds of activities stimulate the happy child, but you need to realise that it does take time. This is the big sticking point for Sarah in particular. She is either hard at work or distracting herself, for example by getting lost on the internet. Of course, she actually is busy with a busy job and a family, but it should be possible to do something fun at least a few times a week. After all, you can also do that together with your partner and your children. You can even organise more relaxation at work by taking a walk or exercising with colleagues during breaks instead of eating lunch at the computer. If you aren't sure what you would want to do yet, just try a few things.

Homework to change your modes independently

Homework is particularly important in this fourth step of changing your modes: you take action independently, ultimately to change your behaviour. The homework corresponds to the topics we have described in this chapter: exercises to gain new experiences, change your thoughts and change your behaviour. We list a few possibilities below, but you can think of other homework on your own or together with your therapist that will help you satisfy your needs better. The homework you agree on in this fourth step is no longer just a recommendation, but you really have to do it, so you can discuss what did and didn't work, and why, with your therapist in the next session. The therapist encourages you more than before, because they know how difficult it is to change behaviour. Old behavioural patterns are deeply ingrained and familiar, but the therapist also knows how much you will gain from striking out on new paths.

To make your intentions concrete, it is helpful to write them down in the 'Homework Form Worksheet' (see Appendix 6).

Gaining new experiences

To gain new experiences, you can try the following exercises at home:

- *Using chairs.* If you have experienced something unpleasant and you find that your critical mode or coping mode threatens to take over, you can use two chairs at home to prevent this. Choose a quiet moment and put one of these modes on one chair and your healthy adult on another chair opposite it. In this way, you can fight and stop those unhelpful modes (see Exercise 6.2).
- *Visualisation exercise.* You can also try the visualisation exercise at home if you have experienced a difficult situation (see 'Intervention by Martin's healthy adult', p. 152). Homework can also include actively engaging with future situations and trying out in your thoughts how you would like to approach them (see p. 157).
- *Writing letters.* You can also express your feelings in a letter to people in the present or from your past (you don't usually send them!) or to yourself (see 'Letter from Martin to Little Martin', p. 184). Letters to other people may contain a negative or a positive message. Perhaps you want to pour out your heart about something that has been done to you, or you feel the need to express other emotions that you cannot share

with someone in person (anymore). The reason why you don't usually send letters with a negative message is because it might make you feel inhibited. You will usually hold back more if you know that someone is going to read it.

Changing thoughts

Take a close look at a minimum of one difficult situation each week by independently filling in *self-inquiry circles* at home (see Exercise 5.5, p. 134) or by keeping a *thought journal* (see Exercise 6.3, p. 171).

If you encounter the same pitfalls and modes regularly, write a healthy message on a *thought card*. You can use this to dispel the thoughts involved in these pitfalls and modes. Write down what your pitfall or mode tells you on the front of the card and the reaction of your healthy adult on the other side. Read such a card regularly and let the message really sink in.

A thought card for Sarah

First, Sarah writes down what 'the Hustler', her demanding mode, confronts her with:

> In situations where performance is key, I often think I can only be satisfied if everything is perfect. If that fails, I see myself as a failure. That's 'the Hustler', who gives me what-for when I make a mistake. He says I should try much harder.

On the other side, she writes the healthy adult's reaction to contradict this:

> It really isn't necessary always to do everything perfectly. If I just do my best, that is good enough. I don't have to work harder than other people. I also have to make time for fun things and relaxation, otherwise I'll get exhausted. Everyone makes a mistake once in a while, including me. That's not a disaster and it doesn't mean I have to try harder.

A third way to combat negative thoughts and reinforce your positive thoughts is to *keep a positive logbook* and possibly to read it out loud to yourself. In a positive logbook, you should preferably write down all the fun and good things you did every day. With this, you also indicate what that says about you as a person and what your good qualities are. It certainly doesn't only have to be about very big things. Giving someone a compliment also belongs in this log. It can also include cooking a nice meal or calling a friend to catch up. The 'Positive Logbook Worksheet' is given in Appendix 7.

Changing behaviour

When you are working on changing your behaviour, try to act from your healthy adult as much as possible. This will help your needs to be met better. That includes learning to deal with your feelings better: on the one hand by accepting them and on the other hand by expressing them in a way that befits the situation.

You gradually change how you relate to your social contacts. You spend more time on people who are good for you. You will distance yourself more from other people or sometimes even cut off contact. It may also be necessary to make new friends. When you start to change, not everyone can easily follow you in this: it takes some getting used to for some people. It often does help to tell others that you are making a change so they understand what is going on and can adjust accordingly.

Behavioural experiment

You can do a behavioural experiment to learn how to handle situations differently. A behavioural experiment is a playful way to learn new things just by doing them, even if you don't think it will go well.

You can prepare for a situation in the near future by describing the new behaviour you want to try out. In preparation, write down what you will do at what moment (as specifically as possible) and predict what you think the effect will be. This prediction is usually coloured by your critical mode to some extent. Afterwards, you evaluate which prediction came true and which did not.

Martin usually adopts a passive attitude in the company of others. As an experiment, he can start a chat every time he meets someone. That could be at work, but also in the train or in a shop. He predicts that many people will react negatively or be uninterested. Sarah can start experimenting with intentionally making mistakes or saying something wrong. She predicts that many people will get angry.

In practice, you will find that the effects are not that negative at all, and you will try out that new behaviour more often.

Trying out new behaviour
Look for ways to relax. Think yoga, mindfulness or other techniques to help you relax and gain perspective – something that you feel good doing.

Start trying new things to strengthen the happy child. At the end of each session, the therapist will discuss what you will try out in the upcoming period. You can use the 'Changing Behavioural Patterns Worksheet' (see Appendix 8) for this.

In each session after that, the therapist will discuss with you what you tried and how it went. If something didn't work out, you will work together to find another approach. And if you do succeed, you should try to stick to this approach and do it this way more often.

Difficult moments

When you start putting what you've discovered about yourself in the previous steps into practice, sticking points usually arise. Behaviour change sometimes happens automatically, but often it does not. I give a few examples of common problems below, using the stories of Sarah, Martin and Nora.

Difficult moments when you start changing your modes on your own

Sarah knows she needs to work less hard. She makes a plan for how to do this and fills in the 'Changing Behavioural Patterns Worksheet' (see Appendix 8). She runs into two problems when she does this. She finds it difficult to stop work on time if not everything is finished (High Demands pitfall). Aside from that, she doesn't really know what to do with her free time if she isn't working as hard (when 'the Hustler' is mostly silent) and not sitting in front of the computer or TV as much.

She will discuss the first problem with a colleague who has suffered from burnout before. She knows that colleague also had help at the time to recover and arrange his work differently. It is a relief for her to share her problem with him. She resolves to put some of this colleague's tips into practice. When she discusses these plans with some friends, she discovers that other people are also struggling with this. Aside from recognition, it also gives her a few more ways to deal with it.

To address the second problem, she resolves to suppress the tendency to immediately start planning everything and just to take more time for small things. She realises that she doesn't need to know exactly what hobbies or activities she will do to fill the freed-up time. That could well be her old pitfall of High Demands: wanting to do too much in too little time. By looking at everything calmly, she discovers how nice it is to be at home relaxing with her family or spending time with friends. Not only does this approach reduce the intensity of her pitfall of High Demands, but also meets her need for contact and understanding (pitfall of Emotional Deprivation) better.

Martin makes a plan for how he wants to organise his week so he has more time to work in the allotment he has recently been able to obtain and spends less time helping others. He makes a plan to say he doesn't have time more often. He also resolves to ask a few people to come and help him in his garden in exchange for his help with a job in their house. He complements 'do good, have good' with 'one good turn deserves another'.

The plan is good, but the therapist notices that Martin is not actually doing it. Together, they discover that Little Martin is still afraid to say no because he thinks people will get angry with him. With the experiential exercises, Martin is reminded again of the source of this fear: his pitfalls Failure and Subjugation. The therapist then does role-plays with him to practise saying no. They fill in the 'Changing Behavioural Patterns Worksheet' together (see Appendix 8). But Martin is still hesitant to put this skill into practice. The therapist has to confront him firmly a few times about the fact that he isn't keeping to the agreement that he will actually change his behaviour pattern.

In the end, Martin does execute his plans. Then he notices that not everyone is enthusiastic about this change. His mother and various acquaintances are only too happy to have his help, so when Martin hits them with 'no', it can be quite a spanner in the works. One of his acquaintances even gets angry and heaps all kinds of blame on him. This is very instructive for Martin because he discovers that he can still refuse to do something in spite of this. When they fail to talk it out, Martin decides to end this relationship. Martin's mother also notices that he isn't always available anymore and finally decides to go to the doctor to discuss her need for help with him.

Meanwhile, Martin is making new friends at the garden. He makes sure there is more reciprocity in these new relationships. He helps others, but they also help him. He is also learning that he can lay out his garden as he likes and doesn't worry as much about what the neighbours think of it (decrease in Dependence and Approval Seeking).

Nora gains more and more self-confidence because more and more things succeed. One day a week, she very much enjoys doing volunteer work with children, and she plans to pursue education for this. She is drinking less alcohol and only occasionally smoking marijuana (increase in

Self-discipline). She has also met new people through the volunteer work. She is less afraid of being abandoned and feels lonely less often (decrease in the pitfalls Abandonment/Instability and Social Isolation/Alienation).

Unfortunately, the problems with Frank persist. She has suggested couples therapy, but he does not want to do that. He fails to find a job. He also has difficulty with the fact that Nora is doing better, let alone supporting her in her new plans. Their quarrels regularly get out of control, with Nora invariably coming off worse. Even so, she always makes up with Frank.

Several times, the therapist discusses with her what exactly makes her continue with this difficult relationship in spite of this. Nora's 'Wall' doesn't like this because it is used to avoiding difficult topics or making jokes about them. However, the therapist insists that this is a serious problem. They use experiential exercises to explore why she is afraid to ask herself certain questions about the relationship. They also do self-inquiry circles and list the pros and cons of continuing the relationship.

When Nora subsequently comes to therapy with a black eye, the therapist strongly urges her to make a change. Apparently 'the Witch' is still saying that it is Nora's fault that the relationship is not working. They put that mode on a chair. Then Nora's healthy adult self combats that mode. This goes quite well. It creates space to come up with a plan to handle this relationship differently. Nora decides to take a three-month break and temporarily moves somewhere else. This will allow her to calmly examine what she wants from her relationship in the future.

Sometimes your new modes have far-reaching implications for your life. These changes are not exclusively

> positive – and certainly not for others. Some of Martin's friends are indignant that he doesn't help them as much anymore. With Sarah not working overtime every time, her supervisor has to find another way to get all the work done. Nora might well decide to end the relationship for good after the break. Frank won't be happy about that. Although you might have to make painful decisions, the long-term effect can be positive for you. You are able to fulfil your needs better and break free from past modes.

∗ ∗ ∗

In this fourth step of changing modes, the main focus was on behavioural change. Now you put everything you learnt in the previous steps into practice, by changing your behaviour. This chapter offers several exercises to help you do this. In both the visualisation exercise and the chair technique, you learn to intervene as a healthy adult yourself instead of your therapist taking on this role. You also use the visualisation exercise to prepare for future difficult situations. You use role-playing to analyse recent situations in which your pitfalls or modes were activated. You can now complete a self-inquiry circle or the thought journal independently. You learnt how to care for your vulnerable child, how to express anger in a balanced way and how to limit your impulsive, undisciplined or spoilt child mode. Finally, you got tips on how to stimulate the healthy adult and the happy child.

In the next chapter about Step 5, the final step of changing modes, you will learn how to retain the changes you have made so your old modes gradually disappear.

Step 4 Overview

Changing your modes independently (usually takes 20–40 weeks)

Section	Therapist	Client	You do it yourself	Friend
Recognising modes	Takes on a coaching role.	Can already recognise modes afterwards or in a given situation by themselves.	You recognise modes.	Becomes slightly less active.
Changing modes	Gives explanation about the method in the fourth step of the treatment.	Reads Chapter 6.	You read Chapter 6.	Reads Chapter 6.
Changing modes at the emotional level	With the coaching attitude, the therapist encourages the healthy adult to intervene themselves.	The healthy adult regularly succeeds in intervening in the visualisation exercise, role-play and chair technique themselves.	You can use a visualisation exercise, role-play and the chair technique if necessary. You increasingly find yourself in the healthy adult mode.	Supports you in making changes.

Changing your modes independently (usually takes 20–40 weeks)

Section	Therapist	Client	You do it yourself	Friend
Changing modes by changing thoughts	Has a coaching role. Discusses the self-inquiry circle or thought journal on request.	Completes self-inquiry circles and thought journals independently at home.	You complete self-inquiry circles and thought journals independently.	Supports you in making changes.
Behavioural change	Encourages trying out new behaviours, whether or not in the form of experiments.	Slowly but surely tries out different behaviour.	You try new behaviours regularly.	Supports you in making changes.
Strengthening the healthy adult	Explains the three steps to bring in the healthy adult.	Practices the three steps to activate the healthy adult.	You practice the three steps to activate the healthy adult.	Supports you in making changes.
Learning to care for the vulnerable child	Encourages Grown-Up Me to take care of Little Me.	Writes a letter to Little Me and takes better care of them.	You write a letter to your little child and take better care of her.	Supports you in making changes.
Expressing anger too much or too little	Explains how to deal with anger in a balanced way.	Practises recognising anger earlier and expressing it in a controlled way.	You practice recognising anger earlier and expressing it as a healthy adult.	Notices that you address her/him differently when you are angry.

Learning to limit the impulsive, undisciplined or spoilt child	Explains how to limit the impulsive, undisciplined or spoilt child.	Practises recognising impulsive, undisciplined or spoilt behaviour earlier and limiting it as a healthy adult.	You practice recognising impulsive, undisciplined or spoilt behaviour earlier and limiting it as a healthy adult.	Supports you in making changes.
Homework	Encourages practicing new behaviour.	Does homework.	You try new behaviours regularly.	Notices that you are changing.
Difficult moments	Notices that the client finds it difficult to reflect on problems in relationships.	Prefers not to talk about problems for fear of the consequences when they are discussed.	You are still struggling with your biggest challenges.	Fills in any points where you have a blind spot.
Tips for difficult moments	Repeatedly confronts client about relationship problems and other sticking points in an empathetic way.	Takes action to address several sticking points in life.	You discuss your persistent pitfall with others and get more support this way.	Can encourage you to implement his or her plan.

7

Step 5: Continuing to change modes in the future

You've already changed a lot, and it is time for the last step. You are increasingly able to be in your healthy adult mode, alternating it with the happy child. Of course, your life still has its problems, and there are still some things you want to address, but you already feel much better. Old modes have faded into the background, but that doesn't mean you never have to pay attention to them again. They can still sometimes rear their heads in difficult situations. Not to the same extent as before, but it does help to be aware of risk factors.

That is why you make a plan to prevent relapse (a relapse prevention plan). You do a few more exercises to further reinforce what you have achieved. You have fewer appointments with your therapist, work on your problems independently and prepare to take leave of your therapist. The friendship with the friend who helped you will also change back into a more equal and reciprocal relationship. This period does not demand as much attention as in the first year because your healthy adult and happy child are much stronger.

Recognising and changing modes early, and identifying triggers

In your daily life now, you usually realise in time when an old pitfall lies in wait. In this step, you prepare yourself for situations where your old modes might resurface. Make sure you regularly set aside time to look to the future. You discuss what you've tried with your therapist every three or four weeks. You bring in what you want to discuss with her, or she might point out a blind spot if something still isn't going as well as hoped. She encourages you to discuss your problems with your partner and close friends from now on, so that she gradually becomes unnecessary.

Gaining new experiences

We already described how to prepare for future (difficult) situations with a visualisation exercise in Chapter 6. You can also do role-playing together with your therapist or friend to prepare for situations, use chairs or write letters.

Role-play

Exercise 7.1 does not look at situations from the (recent) past, but at future situations. Of course, you can't know exactly what these situations will look like concretely when the time comes, but you can try out how you can react in a given scenario.

Exercise 7.1

Future-oriented role-play

Choose a situation you are apprehensive about and ask your therapist to play the role of the other person. Explain to the therapist what you are afraid of (for example the other person getting angry) and ask her to play that. By doing this, you actually practise two skills: how to get a message across in a difficult situation and also how to deal with all kinds of reactions that you have difficulty with. That means you try to say something from healthy adult mode, even if the situation stressful to you. So you deliberately ask your therapist to play an angry response. That allows you to practise staying in the healthy adult, even when the other person reacts angrily.

You can also reverse the roles, as was done in the other role-plays (Exercise 5.3 and Exercise 6.1), but it is not necessary. Role reversal now has a different purpose. For example, the therapist in the role of the other person may notice that you are not at all as clear as you might believe, and might then suggest that you play the other person while the therapist plays you. This way, you will experience for yourself whether you were clear enough.

In the review, you can determine how to handle it better and try it out again.

Part 1

The therapist plays the other person in the situation as realistically as possible or even exaggerates their reaction a little bit. The goal is that you also learn to deal with people who are not that easy going.

Review

After you have re-enacted the situation together, discuss whether your healthy adult was clear enough. Did the therapist (in the role of the other person) clearly understand the message, or perhaps you were too vague or cautious?

Part 2

If you don't know what you did too vaguely or cautiously, the roles are reversed. The therapist plays you and you play the other person. In the role of the other person, you try to understand why your message did not come across clearly.

Review

Afterwards, you discuss which mode likely caused you not to be clear enough and how to improve.

Part 3

You play yourself again and are clearer. The therapist plays the other person involved in the situation as realistically as possible and that can include a sharp or angry reaction.

Review

You discuss what it was like to be really clear and whether you were able to handle a negative reaction.

You cannot predict whether the interaction will actually be like this in the future. However, what you can learn from this exercise is how to handle this kind of situation from your healthy adult perspective.

Future-oriented role-play exercise with Nora

After several attempts to improve her relationship with Frank, Nora has reached her limit. She wants to tell him that she will live separately from him for a while to examine whether, and if so how, she wants to move forward with the relationship. She is afraid that Frank will be furious. They agree that the therapist will react angrily in the role of Frank.

Part 1

N: Frank, I have to tell you something. You might not like this, but I need to take some time to find peace.

T: What do you mean, are you going on holiday?

N: No, I have the opportunity to move into Olivia's house for three months because she's going on a long trip and needs someone to look after the cats.

T: (slightly angry) Why do you have to you to go live there? She lives nearby. Can't you take care of the cats from here?

The therapist interrupts the role-play and indicates that she (as Frank) does not understand why Nora wants to leave for three months.

Part 2

They reverse the roles and the therapist repeats what Nora has just said. Nora plays Frank. With this, she discovers that her tendency to avoid difficult matters ('the Wall') causes her to skirt around the issue and use the cats as an argument.

She resolves that now she will say the reason why she wants to leave for three months.

Part 3

Nora tries the role-play again, but this time from her healthy adult point of view.

N: Frank, I have to tell you something. I think we argue far too often and we are not making any progress in our relationship. I don't know how to go forward. So I've decided to live apart for three months to think about my future.

T: (slightly angry) What kind of nonsense is that? We always make up, don't we?

N: We do, but nothing changes. You don't usually do your chores around the house. You still go out with your friends without mentioning it to me. And there are other things that I can't stand anymore. I need more attention and to do things together, but that still isn't happening.

T: (angry) You're exaggerating and blaming me for everything.

N: I'm trying to explain it to you calmly and I'm annoyed that you are starting to get so angry now. I might have my part to play as well, but I'll go and think about that on my own. I'd like you to do that in this time too.

T: (very angry) You do what you have to do, but I think it's idiotic.

After this, they discuss what went well and what did not go well in this role-play. The key concerns are whether Nora has now been able to say what she needs and whether she has had enough practise responding to an angry Frank. If this is not quite yet achieved, they can do the role-play again until they are both satisfied with the result.

Using chairs

So far, we have always used the chair technique to recognise and then change your modes. You can also use chairs to actively practise going against your critical mode or coping mode. You then ask the therapist to play those modes in a very exaggerated way.

Exercise 7.2

Using chairs to strengthen countcracting old modes

The therapist or your friend sits in the chair of your critical mode or coping mode. She deliberately plays that mode rather exaggeratedly to have you practice going against it.

You sit in the chair opposite and refute all the arguments of that mode as forcefully as possible. The other person gives counterarguments in turn and persists in playing that critical or coping mode for as long as possible until she can no longer stand up to your arguments.

Using chairs to go against your old modes with Martin

Martin still has difficulty saying no to his friends, especially when someone asks him something in a plaintive tone. The therapist suggests that he can play 'the Feeling of Guilt' evoked by someone like that. Martin has to try to stand by his decision and go against 'the Feeling of Guilt'. Martin mentions an acquaintance who often asks for his help. They sit facing each other in two chairs. The therapist deliberately exaggerates and tries to hold out for as long as possible.

T: You really need to go help George because he really needs your help. It'll be way too difficult for him to do everything on his own.

M: That's too bad for George, but surely he has other people who can help him?

T: No, not really, because you're so handy and others aren't.

M: I really don't have time to help him with this job. He'll just have to find someone else.

T: But surely you can just make an hour free somewhere? You're on your own anyway and you don't have a family to take care of.

M: That has nothing to do with it. I have a busy job and very much need my free time.

The therapist steps out of his role for a moment to compliment Martin for holding up well. The therapist suggests that Martin should say something about the fact that 'the Feeling of Guilt' keeps pressing.

T: Yes, but he really won't manage it without your help.

M: I notice that, as the Feeling of Guilt, you aren't actually listening to my arguments. I'm done with

> this. I can't help him this time. I'm going to end the
> conversation now.
> T: (angry tone) So you're not listening to me!
> M: Indeed, that's enough. Now I'm going to keep doing
>   what I was busy with.
>
> The therapist stops objecting and notes that he has run out of
> arguments. Martin has experienced what it is like to stand
> firm in a difficult situation. He is quite happy about that.

Writing letters

In addition to the experiential exercises from Step 3 (Chapter 5), another way to process traumatic experiences is to give your emotions a place in a letter to someone who is responsible for them. This could even be someone who has already died. You don't usually send this kind of letter. The aim is not to start a dialogue, but simply to express your feelings about what that person has done to you. You write these kinds of letters to people who are unable or unwilling to talk to you about their behaviour. Because you don't send the letter, you don't have to hold back. However, if you want to, you can read the letter to your therapist or someone else you trust. This reinforces the effect.

Changing thoughts

In this phase of the treatment, you are probably not wrestling that hard with negative thoughts anymore. It usually comes naturally to you to negate them. If something really serious happens in your life, you will look for ways to help you fulfil your needs in those difficult circumstances, for instance to share your grief or express your anger. In such cases, you might consider completing a thought journal (Exercise 6.3) or doing a self-inquiry circle (Exercise 5.5). You can also keep a regular diary in which you write down what you have experienced and what you feel and think in the process. In this way, you not only come up with helpful thoughts, but you might also discover what you could do to change the situation.

Changing behaviour

If the people around you do not change along with you, or even work against you, you will fall back into old modes more easily. In that case, you sometimes have to take a big step to change your modes permanently. For instance, it might be necessary for younger people to move out and go live independently if their parents are the most important cause of their modes. A relationship with a partner who cannot or will not satisfy your needs also hinders your future development. The same applies to an unhealthy working environment.

It is always advisable to try something to get people around you on board first. You can tell them that you are changing your modes and explain that it will be noticeable in your behaviour in some areas. Also try to explain what your needs are and ask if the other person can understand that. If that doesn't help enough, you can ask for additional help. In case of relationship problems, for example your partner can come along to the sessions with your therapist a few times or you can go into couples therapy together. If you have problems at work, you can consult a coach or look for someone within the company who can help you. But sometimes your efforts don't have enough effect and then you might have to draw your own conclusions.

It is not recommended to make major changes yet after the first steps in the process of changing modes. It is better to wait until your healthy adult is developed enough that you can make a considered decision. This should not be done from a child mode, which primarily makes decisions based on your emotions. A critical mode or a coping mode is also a poor advisor when it comes to major changes in your life.

Planning big changes

In the final phase of changing your modes, there is no longer any real homework. You try to apply everything you have learnt in daily practice as well as you can. For major changes, it does still make sense to make an action plan. Of course, you don't meet a new partner just like that, and you don't automatically find a new job either. For example, you can find out how other people have approached these things. Then you plan a regular time, for example weekly or daily, to work on your plans. It can be good to discuss your plans with someone you trust.

You are preparing for the fact that, not too long from now, you will be doing everything without a therapist.

Big changes for Nora, Martin and Sarah

After living apart from Frank for several months, Nora decides to break off the relationship. She has noticed that she is much calmer when she is alone. She has also met other people through her education who align much better with her needs. The therapist advises her to build a life on her own first and not to start a new relationship right away. She explains to Nora that it is better for her to take the time to develop her healthy adult further. One way she can do this is by expanding her circle of friends with trustworthy and caring people.

Martin is spending more and more time doing things he enjoys. He has made new friends at the allotment and other places as well, who he does fun things with. He has joined organised trips a couple of times. He increasingly feels that he would actually like to find a new partner. That is very daunting for him because he's afraid of becoming too dependent on someone else again. The therapist suggests that he does take action in that area, but not to rush things when he meets someone he likes. Together, they draw up a list of his basic needs and vulnerabilities. A partner who is too critical or wants him to dance to her tune would revive 'the Strict One' or 'the Feeling of Guilt'. So he goes looking for a relationship where his autonomy and independence are adequately guaranteed. It is also important that he feels seen, appreciated and recognised.

Sarah is having a number of conversations with a coach to figure out what she likes and doesn't like about her job and how she can change certain things. She proposes several changes in her job and working hours, but her supervisor does not want to cooperate. Eventually, she comes to the conclusion that she had better look for a different job that is more suited to her interests and abilities. She takes great care to make sure it is a working environment with fewer High Demands and a good atmosphere.

A plan to prevent relapse

If you have done all the steps well, the chances are not very high that you will completely fall back into your old modes in the future. However, it is a good idea to make a plan in advance in case something serious unexpectedly happens in your life, such as losing your job, divorce or the death of a loved one. Consider the following points when making a plan to prevent relapse:

1. The most important thing is that you know what needs were not met earlier in your life and therefore where your bruises are. When something happens that upsets you, the first thing to do is to activate the three aspects of the healthy adult:
   - acknowledge the feeling (be gentle and kind to yourself)
   - contradict negative thoughts (which thoughts do help?)
   - figure out what you can do.
2. Write down who you can ask for help or support. If everything has gone well, a few friends or family members are

aware of your old modes and they know how hard you have worked to change them. They also know that, once in a while, you can use some extra support when things get tough.

3. Don't let problems deteriorate until you feel really bad. Get support from others in time.

4. Be realistic about what is possible. You will not always be able to be balanced and solve every problem quickly. Everyone experiences things that throw them off balance from time to time. Consider your abilities and limitations on a personal, social and societal level. Unfortunately, some situations cannot be changed. For example, you can't change your family, so you might have to distance yourself from them a bit more than before.

5. Keep the notes, worksheets and other forms that you used during your change process or therapy. Use them to help you when you experience something hard.

6. Make an agreement with your therapist about what you can do if you don't manage to solve your problems on your own. In many cases, a therapist will tell you that you can contact her in the future if you are really struggling.

Of course, it is not that life will never have its challenges again. The goal of changing modes is not that you'll be happy all the time from now on. But if something unpleasant or even very serious happens in your life, you now have a better ability to deal with it in a healthy way. You know what your vulnerable modes are and can usually make sure that the healthy adult remains the captain of your ship. And now you probably have more people around you who will support you and help you when you need it.

Difficult moments

Some problems do not have an immediate solution, and sometimes you have to be very patient or even accept that something cannot be changed. It can also be difficult to take leave of your therapist. The difficult moments for Nora, Martin and Sarah are illustrative of common difficulties in completing the final step.

Difficult moments when you continue changing modes in the future

Nora finds it hard to say goodbye to her therapist now that she has just broken off her relationship. She has a lot to deal with after the break-up. The therapist assures her that she is confident that Nora can cope on her own from now on. Nora asks if she can contact her again in the future. The therapist says that this is alright as long as she has implemented her relapse prevention plan first. The therapist suggests that they see each other again in six months in any case, so she can hear about how Nora is doing. That prospect gives Nora a little more peace and courage to go it alone.

In the final appointments, they pay attention to taking leave in a positive way because taking leave does somewhat reactivate Nora's fear of the Abandonment/Instability pitfall.

Martin would prefer to stay in therapy until he finds a new partner. He is still afraid that he will fall for the wrong woman again. He falls a little bit back into his dependent behaviour towards the therapist. The therapist insists on the plan to stop therapy after two years. Together, they make a plan to prevent relapse. The therapist does suggest that Martin can come back for two more sessions in the future if he is unsure about his choice of partner. This is on the condition that he reviews his list of needs and vulnerabilities himself first. First, he can look independently at the points on which a possible new partner may or may not suit him.

In the final appointments, they pay attention to taking leave in a positive way because every goodbye activates the Dependence/Incompetence pitfall for Martin.

Sarah wants to change the relationship with the friend who has often helped her. Over the past year, that relationship has grown a bit lopsided in the sense that it was always about her problems and never about her friend. Sarah wants a more equal relationship.

To her surprise, this is very difficult for her friend. At first, her friend denies that she also has problems at times. Sarah knows this is not true and mentions a couple of examples. Her friend does not find this easy to admit. She has a bit of a Self-Sacrifice pitfall herself. She likes to be there for others and derives a sense of importance from this. If the roles are reversed, she becomes insecure. Because reading this book has also sometimes made the friend think about her own modes, she can still talk to Sarah about it and they work it out together.

* * *

In this last step, you learnt how to avoid falling back into old modes. It is important to realise at an early stage that an old mode is threatening to resurface. You can prepare for the future using a role-play focused on future situations, firmly reiterating the arguments against your critical and coping modes and writing letters. If everything has gone well, you already fight negative thoughts automatically.

Even after Step 5, keep making sure that the healthy adult remains the captain of your ship. To do this, make a plan to prevent relapse. When life is tough, this can already be very helpful in handling your problems.

Sometimes it is necessary to make big changes in your life. You have changed step by step, and most people will accept or even appreciate the changes in your modes, but not everyone. You take leave of your therapist and the friend who helped you takes a different role in your life.

Step 5 Overview

Continuing to change modes in the future (usually takes 10–18 weeks)

Section	Therapist	Client	You do it yourself	Friend
Recognising modes and triggers in the future	Takes on a coaching role.	Can analyse future situations in which modes could be triggered.	You think about future choices and changes.	Supports you in this process of making choices.
Changing modes at the emotional level	Encourages client to do visualisation exercises about the future. Plays people with whom the client is in a difficult situation or persistent modes.	Should be able to do a visualisation exercise on their own. Practises going against people she or he is in a difficult situation with, and against persistent modes.	You try out experiential techniques with a focus on the future. You do role-plays and use the chair technique to counteract persistent modes.	Role increasingly changes back to that of friend, with both supporting each other.
Changing modes by changing thoughts	Encourages client to discover logical errors on their own.	Has fewer unhelpful thoughts. Changing thoughts is increasingly automatic.	You have fewer unhelpful thoughts. Changing thoughts is increasingly automatic.	Role increasingly changes back to that of friend, with both supporting each other.

Behavioural change	Is vigilant that certain changes are not avoided.	She/he is often able to adopt new behaviours. Can reward themselves for that. Prepares for possible major changes in relationships and professional life.	You are often able to adopt new behaviour and can reward yourself for this. You prepare for possible major changes in your relationships and professional life.	Supports you in the process of making choices.
Planning big changes	Supports plans to try things out. Pays attention to basic needs being fulfilled when doing this.	Decides what he/she wants to try out themselves. Discussion with family members if necessary. Notices the positive effect of different behaviour.	Homework is no longer that necessary. You do make sure that you actually carry out your intentions.	
Difficult moments	Mentions the farewell and prepares for it together with client.	Makes a relapse prevention plan.	You make a relapse prevention plan.	Looks at the plan. Adds to it if necessary.
Tips	Makes it clear that relapse does not mean client is back to square one.	Works on retaining changes. Asks for help when the going gets tough.	You work on retaining changes.	Ceases playing the role of helper.

8

In conclusion

Changing your modes in five steps is an intensive process that can help you make a significant change to problematic modes. Just figuring out which modes are causing you problems gives some relief from your symptoms (Step 1, Chapter 3). Most people report that it is a relief to understand yourself better and to realise that it is not all your fault. You discover the influence your parents, other caregivers or peers have had on the formation of your modes. Discovering modes within yourself can be enlightening, and recognising modes in people around you can lead to greater understanding of others.

It is best to go through the five steps in this book together with someone else. This could be a friend or a therapist, depending on how the degree to which you suffer from your modes. The other person can support you in difficult moments and point out your blind spots.

But it is not always necessary to engage a schema therapist. If you notice that you do have persistent modes that come up from time to time at difficult moments in your life, but that they don't determine everything you do, you can try it yourself first.

If you are using this book as a self-help book, it is important to go through the steps in the right order. When doing this, also use the worksheets that accompany each chapter. If you could still use some support when you do this, you can often turn to a counsellor working in primary mental health care or connected to your family doctor's practice. Or, like Sarah in this book, you enlist the help of one or more friends.

But if many basic needs have gone unfulfilled in your life and you had many traumatic experiences in your childhood, you will probably find that you can't get out of it on your own. It is not a good idea to burden a friend with such serious problems either. In that case, it is definitely worthwhile to engage a schema therapist. A schema therapist has undergone extensive psychotherapeutic training before training as a schema therapist. That gives them much more experience and knowledge about personality problems. You can easily find a schema therapist with the right training at www.schematherpysociety.com.

Once you know what modes you have, the next step to change is to start recognising when your modes are giving you problems (Step 2, Chapter 4: *Recognising modes in everyday situations*) and the ways to change your modes (Step 3, Chapter 5: *Starting to change modes*). You discover that there are three ways to do this:

1. Gaining new experiences (feeling)
2. Changing thoughts (thinking)
3. Changing behaviour (doing)

All three ways are relevant, so apply all three. If all goes well, your schema therapist will also use all these methods. You will discover which way suits you best as you work on it. But, for example, don't stop when you start feeling a bit better and thinking more positively, but also work on actually changing your behaviour. Changing your behaviour is described in detail in Step 4, Chapter 6: *Changing your modes independently*. This step is not easy because although people around you usually respond positively to your changing behaviour, sometimes they do not. Keep going and seek support from the people who do appreciate the changes you are making.

Finally, it is good to realise that changing your modes is something you need to keep repeating when you face setbacks in the future. Your modes may have changed, but old modes can sometimes return if you are thrown off balance. Recognising and changing modes early, and exploring triggers in the future, is therefore the final step (Step 5, Chapter 7: *Continuing to change modes in the future*). Keep your notes and completed worksheets because you might still need them in the future.

You will definitely feel better once you have gone through these five steps to change your modes. Of course, this does not mean that you will never feel bad again and always be happy. Perhaps you are making fundamental decisions right now to change things in your life. After all, now you know better what your needs are. While a major change (like breaking up a relationship or changing jobs) is probably better for you in the longer term, it can cause pain and grief in the short term. You can also experience unpleasant things, which you had not anticipated, that substantially throw you off balance.

But now you can apply what you have learnt, and you know how you might handle difficult problems. If you still manage to remain the captain of your ship in a big storm, you will find that you can adapt to new situations. With this, it also usually takes less time to regain your balance and move on with your life. In short, all the effort you have made to persevere has not been in vain.

Appendix 1

Mode model worksheet

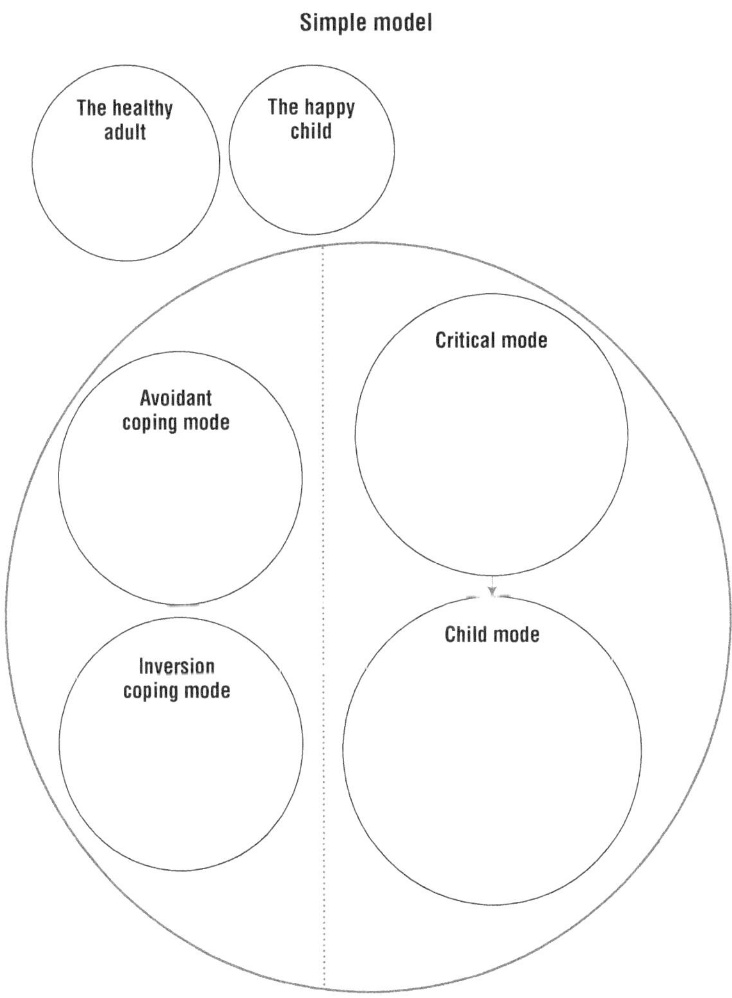

Complex model

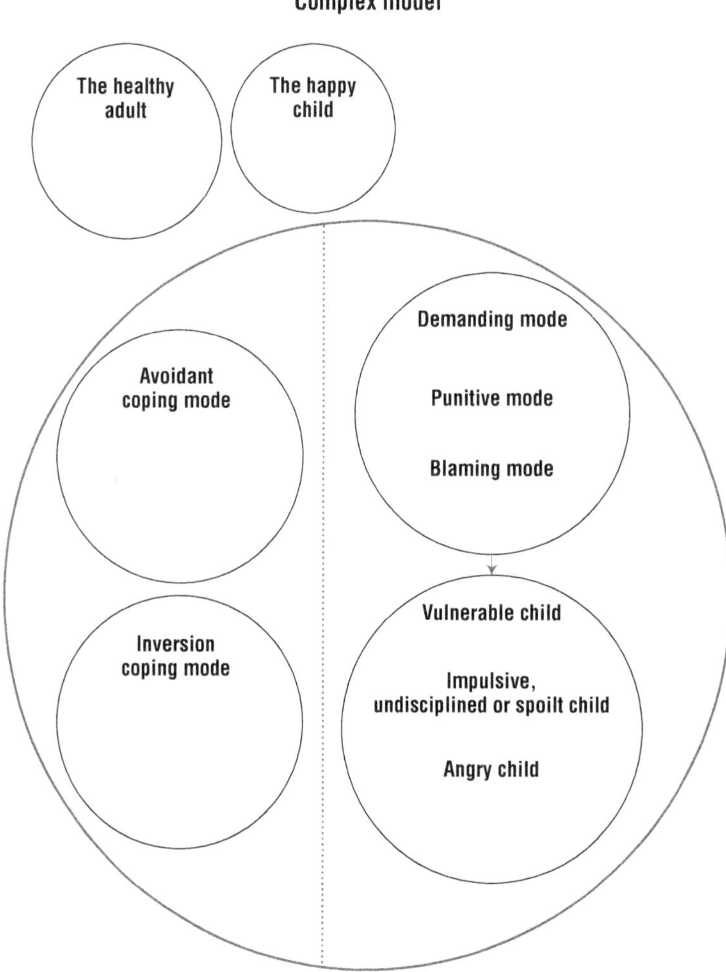

This worksheet can be downloaded at https://www.wiley.com/go/breakingnegativepatterns/1e

Appendix 2

Self-inquiry circle worksheet

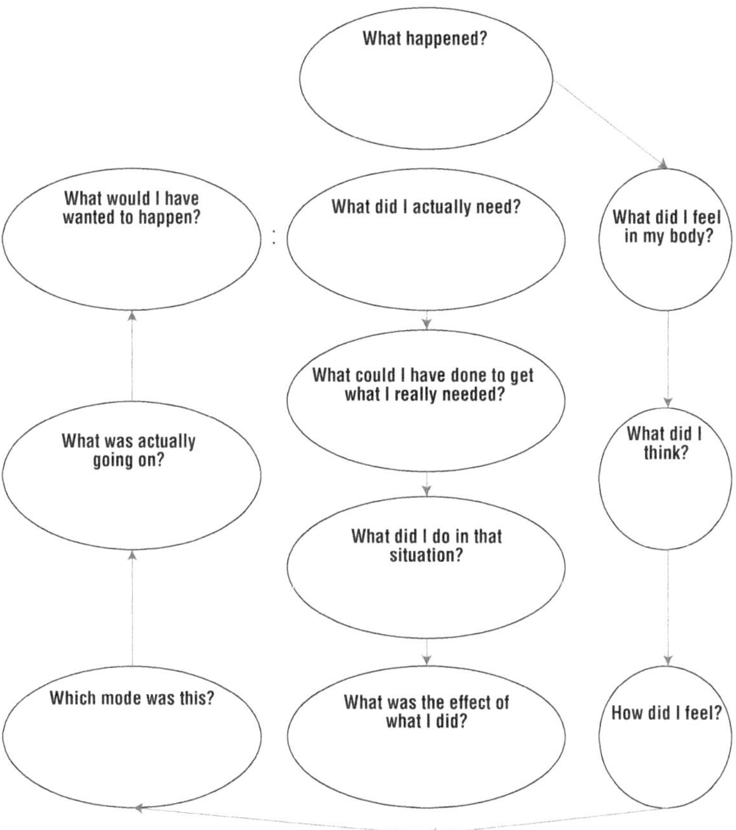

This worksheet can be downloaded at https://www.wiley.com/go/breakingnegativepatterns/1e

Appendix 3

Thought journal worksheet

<table>
<tr><td>

Event (What happened and what provoked my reaction?)

</td></tr>
<tr><td>

Feeling (How did I feel?)

</td></tr>
<tr><td>

Thought (What did I think?)

</td></tr>
<tr><td>

Behaviour (What did I do?)

</td></tr>
<tr><td>

Which of my modes played a role in this?

1. *Child mode:*
2. *Critical mode:*
3. *Coping mode:*
4. *Healthy adult mode:*
5. *Happy child mode:*

</td></tr>
<tr><td>

Which part of my response was justified?

</td></tr>
</table>

Which part of my response was too strong?   *What did one (or more) of my modes do that made it worse?*   *What thoughts will I investigate?*
What would be a better way to look at it?   *What could I do better to resolve the problem?*
New feeling:

This worksheet can be downloaded at https://www.wiley.com/go/breakingnegativepatterns/1e

Appendix 4

Visualisation exercise worksheet

Visualisation of a pleasant situation
Visualisation of unpleasant situations in the present
Visualisation of unpleasant situations in the past
Intervening in the unpleasant situation: Who did what?
Intervening in the unpleasant situation: How were you comforted and supported?

Making connections between past and present

Which basic need was not fulfilled?

Which mode played a role in this?

What was the effect of this on the present situation?

How was my basic need now fulfilled?

This worksheet can be downloaded at https://www.wiley.com/go/breakingnegativepatterns/1e

Appendix 5

Role-play worksheet

Role-play 1	You play yourself as a child The therapist plays the other person (often a parent)	Re-enact the original event
Review	What does the re-enacted event say about me?	
	What do I think the other person thinks about me?	
Role-play 2	You play the other person The therapist plays you as a child	Re-enact the original event, but this time reverse the roles
Review	What did I discover when I played the other person?	
	New insight into what the re-enacted event says about me	
	New insight into what I think the other person thinks about me	

Role-play 3	You play yourself as a child The therapist plays the other person	Re-enact the original event, but now try out a different reaction
Review	What did I discover by trying out a different reaction?	
	New insight into what the re-enacted event says about me	
	New insight into what I think the other person thinks about me	
	Intentions for new behaviour in the future	

This worksheet can be downloaded at https://www.wiley.com/go/breakingnegativepatterns/1e

Appendix 6

Homework form worksheet

<table>
<tr><td>What homework will I do?</td></tr>
<tr><td>When will I do the homework?</td></tr>
<tr><td>What problems in putting it into practice can I think of beforehand?

1.

2.

3.</td></tr>
<tr><td>Ways to solve these problems:

1.

2.

3.</td></tr>
</table>

<table>
<tr><td>Result:</td></tr>
<tr><td>Effect on the modes:</td></tr>
<tr><td>What problems did I not foresee and how did I address them?</td></tr>
</table>

Appendix 7

Positive logbook worksheet

<table>
<tr><td>Try writing down one or more small or large activities or experiences every day that contribute to a positive image of yourself and others. All this information can be used to weaken the critical modes and strengthen the healthy adult mode.</td></tr>
<tr><td>Date:
Subject:</td></tr>
<tr><td>Date:
Subject:</td></tr>
<tr><td>Date:
Subject:</td></tr>
<tr><td>Date:
Subject:</td></tr>
</table>

<table>
<tr><td>

Date:
Subject:

</td></tr>
<tr><td>

Date:
Subject:

</td></tr>
<tr><td>

Date:
Subject:

</td></tr>
</table>

This worksheet can be downloaded at https://www.wiley.com/go/breakingnegativepatterns/1e
Derived from: *Schema Therapy for Borderline Personality Disorder* by Arnoud Arntz &
Hannie van Genderen, published by John Wiley & Sons Ltd. in 2021.

Appendix 8

Changing behavioural patterns worksheet

What behavioural pattern do I want to change?
In which situations does this behaviour often occur?
What do I do in those situations that make things go badly?
What pitfall or mode plays a central role in this?
What arguments are there against this pitfall or mode?
What new behaviour is more effective in these situations?
How did it go when applying new behaviour?

What is the effect on unhelpful modes?
What is the effect on helpful modes?

Bibliography

American Psychiatric Association (2022). *Handboek voor de classificatie van psychische stoornissen* [Diagnostic and Statistical Manual of Mental Disorders] (DSM-5-TR). Amsterdam: Boom Uitgevers.

Arntz, A., Rijkeboer, M., Chan, E., Fassbinder, E. Karaosmanoglu, A., Lee, C.W., & Panzeri, M. (2021). Towards a Reformulated Theory Underlying Schema Therapy: Position Paper of an International Workgroup. *Cognitive Therapy and Research*, 45, 1007–1020. https://doi.org/10.1007/s10608-021-10209-5.

Genderen, H. van, & Arntz, A. (2021). *Schematherapie bij borderline persoonlijkheidsstoornis* [Schema Therapy for Borderline Personality Disorder] (second, fully revised edition). Amsterdam: Uitgeverij Nieuwezijds.

Genderen, H. van, Jacob, G., & Seebauer, L. (2023). *Patronen doorbreken – Negatieve gevoelens en gewoonten herkennen en veranderen* [Breaking Negative Thinking Patterns: A Schema Therapy Self-Help and Support Book] (second updated edition). Amsterdam: Uitgeverij Nieuwezijds.

Jacob, G., & Arntz, A. (2012). *Schematherapie – een praktische handleiding* [Schema Therapy in Practice]. Amsterdam: Uitgeverij Nieuwezijds.

Wijngaart, R. van der (2020). *Imaginaire rescripting, theorie en praktijk* [Imagery Rescripting: Theory and Practice]. Houten: Bohn Stafleu van Loghum.

Wijngaart, R. van der (2022). *Stoelentechniek – theorie en praktijk* [Chairwork: Theory and Practice]. Houten: Bohn Stafleu van Loghum.

Wijngaart, R. van der, & Genderen, H. van (2024). *Schematherapie voor Cluster C-persoonlijkheidsstoornissen* [Schema Therapy for Cluster C Personality Disorders]. Houten: Bohn Stafleu van Loghum.

Young, J.E., & Klosko, J.S. (1999). *Leven in je leven. Leer de valkuilen in je leven kennen* [Reinventing Your Life]. Lisse: Swets & Zeitlinger.
Young, J.E., Klosko, J.S., & Weishaar, M.E. (2005). *Schemagerichte therapie. Handboek voor therapeuten* [Schema Therapy. A Practitioner's Guide]. Houten: Bohn Stafleu van Loghum.

Index